Welcome to the successful world of Wing-shooting!

Birds on the wing,
Are a beauty thing.
Wings gripping air,
Causing us to stare.

Is it a Teal or a Pin?
Is it a drake or a hen?
Lure it with your call,
Give the chase your all.

Aim with perfection,
In the right direction.
Take a LEAD just right,
And it is yours that night.

Few know the solid fun,
The hunt soothes each one.
It's not killing we desire,
But to be one with nature.

After all, the rhyme isn't everything!

Emmitt J. Nelson, 1998

"Wing Shooting LEAD"

Third Edition – February 2004

© Emmitt J. Nelson, President,
Nelson Consulting, Inc.

Published by Nelson Consulting, Inc.
10031 Briar Drive
Houston, TX 77042

Printed in the United States of America

ISBN 0-9664896-7-5

Wing

Shooting

LEAD

Help for shooting a shotgun is now a reality with this new and revolutionary guide to good wing shooting. What you need to know most of all is "how much" to LEAD the target. This book tells all and makes good wing shooting possible for anyone.

Preface:

Shotguns, Wing Shooting and English

When writing about shooting shotguns and shot-shells and hitting a flying target, the English word spelled **"l-e-a-d"** has two different meaning.

The first meaning, "lead" (pronounced **"led"** with a short "e" like in **bed**) is a metal with a specific gravity 11.35, (or 11.35 times heavier than water) used in the manufacture of shot-shell pellets and fishing sinkers and a host of other things.

The second meaning, "lead" (pronounced **"leed"** with a long "e" like in **seed**) is the distance I aim or point the muzzle of my shotgun in front of a flying bird in order to be a successful wing shooter.

In this book I will be using "lead or Lead" for the metal and "LEAD" (CAPITALIZED) meaning the LEAD aiming distance.

Another conflict in words in the world of shooting and shot-shells comes when we use the word "shot." SHOT is used as a verb (She is a good shot.) and as a noun (The shot pattern spreads.) In the latter case referring to the pellets of the shot-shell as they depart the gun muzzle. In most cases when I am referring to Lead, Steel, Hevy Shot or Bismuth shot I use the word "pellet" in conjunction. Otherwise, I'll leave it to the reader to decide which is which.

What is the proper spelling of the words "wing shooting?" Is the spelling "wing-shooting" also correct? I hope so, for I have used both! Can I also use the term "wing-shooter?" I hope I can because I have!

Regarding shooting sports such as using clay pigeons or other target material I simply use the term "bird" to cover all these aspects of shooting at moving air-born targets. To some degree where Sporting Clays operations use targets scooting along the ground, a LEAD is still required. The rules still apply but the speed may be a hard to figure out if you decide and use the LEAD-O-TABLEs.

Table of Contents

Chapter   **Page**

Table of Contents - continued

Figure your
Wing Shooting "LEAD"

From

"LEAD-O-TABLES"
Published by
Nelson Consulting, Inc.
10031 Briar Drive
Houston, Texas 77042

Wing Shooting "LEAD"

Wing Shooting "LEAD"

Chapter 1 - How Much LEAD? Now You Can Know!

Most all shooters have read in magazine articles or chapters in a hunting book about the subject of "How to LEAD" a bird (real or clay) in wing-shooting. Seldom, however, does one see the subject of "How much to LEAD" addressed; so we all ask ourselves, "HOW MUCH DO I LEAD a bird in wing shooting?"

This book tackles this very often written about subject of LEAD from an entirely NEW perspective! In 40 years I have seen little effective work. Sports publications seldom deal with this critical unknown in wing shooting. I believe the reason is most sports writers or other folks who write about shotguns and bird hunting is just like us. In a very specific sense, they do not know the LEAD either.

Some shooter/writers have perfected the art of telling you how they do it. All mostly fail in their effort to instruct you how much to LEAD. Many of them are very fine wing shots, some even expert. But the "factual knowing" of LEAD required can be acquired best by calculating LEAD using simple formulas out of an algebra or physics text book. LEAD is a technical problem dependent on the Laws of Engineering and Physics. So being an engineer and technically educated I see "Wing Shooting LEAD" as a problem in mathematics that has a solution.

Did you know that EXACT LEAD for aiming a shotgun at a flying object is a function of dozens of variables? LEAD depends on the variables of powder type and load, pellet weight, diameter and metal type, shot-shell configuration and gauge, the gun, barrel length and choke, target velocity and weather condition and last but not least the shooter. This being the case, for the average shooter, it is easy to see how no one has effectively tackled the complex subject of LEAD. No one has tried to offer a simplified explanation of the question; "Just how much LEAD do I hold on the bird?"

The good news is that most all of the above variables affect shotgun shooting LEAD so little in the typical field situation that we don't have to worry about them. In fact there are only six variables that are really important in determining the IDEAL LEAD to be held in a well-aimed shot at a flying bird.

These six are:
1. Shot pellet muzzle velocity (energy)
2. Pellet weight - (energy)
3. Pellet diameter - (wind resistance)
4. Bird speed
5. Distance to the bird
6. Wind conditions

The reason these six are the only factors that are important is the shot pellet pattern, spreading as it travels toward the target makes mute all other variables. Even their combined effect is not enough to move the appropriate aiming point (LEAD) more than a few inches. As a practical matter, the shot pellet pattern phenomenon as it spreads larger and larger as it moves toward the target erases the need to consider all variables other than those listed above. I call the pellet spread the "shot-gunner's best friend."

So we can deal appropriately with the above six within the Laws of Engineering and Physics and calculate an IDEAL LEAD. Once we have this LEAD calculated in feet, whether it is three feet or 14 feet we are well on our way to wing shooting success. A LEAD thus determined will not be changed sufficiently enough even if we were to consider all other variables added together, to warrant a corresponding correction in this IDEAL LEAD we will be discussing here. Yes, the spreading pattern of shot becomes our shooting friend. It's true; the answers to all your shot-gunning LEAD questions are right here in your hands in the form of tables called LEAD-O-TABLES. There are enough tables to cover most all shot-shell loads you are apt to use.

Chapter 2 - All the Questions

Sports enthusiasts who love "wing-shooting," come in two basic categories with the first being the greatest in number. These are:

    a: Those who hunt and shoot infrequently and miss a lot and

    b: Those who are excellent to very good; who are proficient through frequent outings and practice sessions.

This book can help both types "a" and "b" shooters, but it will help type "a" by far the greatest amount.

2.1 For "a" - the Infrequent Shooter

If your problem is found in one of the following questions:

- Missing all those easy wing shots?
- Can't figure how much LEAD to hold?
- No one seems to be able to help?

Then try these new and revolutionary LEAD-O-TABLES! You too can become an effective wing shot. How much do you LEAD that target; dove, duck, goose or clay? LEAD-O-TABLES will answer that question.

Most shooters can estimate speeds and distances. This is all you have to start doing in order to become that great wing shot you have always wanted to be. Some readers of "Wing Shooting LEAD" will already be proficient at making these estimates. Others will have to begin to notice flying birds on these terms; "how far is it from me in yards" and "how fast is it flying in miles per hour?"

This will take a little practice and discussion with your hunting partners. One thing you know for sure, a flying bird has a speed. Some are slow and others are very fast. I have a paragraph later in the book that discusses the flying speeds of common game birds. Refer to it and work off these observed speeds to generate your own experience base.

2.2 For "b" the Frequent Shooter

Most of the shooters in this category already have a very high percentage of "hits" or kills. My experience in discussing the LEAD-O-TABLEs with them has shown that the TABLEs become a matter of verification. They typically say after referring to the

TABLEs; "Yes, that is about how much I LEAD in that situation, (bird speed and shot velocity)."

So for both the infrequent and the frequent shooter the questions are the same. The frequent shooter has mastered the art but the infrequent shooter must work a little harder to reach reasonable proficiency.

All the information we need to use the LEAD-O-TABLEs is available by answering the following questions -
- What is the muzzle velocity of the shot-shell I am using?
- How fast is the bird flying?
- How far is that bird from my gun muzzle?

Once you do your estimating and apply them to the appropriate LEAD-O-TABLE you have a LEAD to try. These LEADs are based on easily understood Laws of Engineering and Physics. The new LEAD-O-TABLEs will give you more confidence in your aiming and shooting abilities! Simply determine the type of shot-shell you are using (field load, magnum load or high velocity load), estimate the speed of the bird in "miles per hour" and the distance to the bird in "yards" and read the "Ideal LEAD" right off the LEAD-O-TABLE and give it a try. Adjust a little, as you shoot and wing-shooting success will be yours also.

If you don't want to read about how the LEAD-O-TABLEs came into being right now but want to go right to the tables then turn to Page 86 and get the instructions on how to read the tables.

But please come back when you have time and have a little fun reading about a country boy who grew up shot-gunning for birds and the fun days he had doing it. And how he solved the frustration of not knowing how much to LEAD a flying bird.

Chapter 3 - Shot-gunning for Birds

Taking birds in flight with a shotgun has, almost since the invention of the muzzle-loading shotgun been classified as a sport, first in Europe then later in America. In early America shot-gunning for upland game birds and waterfowl has been popular with hunters and gun enthusiasts for at least 200 years. But at first, at least in America, there often was not a lot of sport involved.

For instance, in the late 1800's the use of wild game was prevalent in the meat supply industry. Professional hunters made their living supplying the buyers working out of the larger cities of the east and mid-west. Each year millions of wild birds were shipped, iced in barrels, to the meat distributors then to the consumer. These birds were supplied by an industry that arose to meet this demand. The professional hunter took all birds he could kill by whatever means without regard to what we know today as sportsmanship. Millions of game birds were killed for food each year.

Then the early American settlers, needing meat for food, typically took every advantage of the game that was available to fulfill this most basic human need.

In early America sportsmanship was a distant second to "feed the family." In my own family I can still distinctly remember my Grandfather Robert Emmitt McNutt telling me of the time he was hunting Geese on the Brazos River near Weatherford, Texas. This would have been during the period 1900 to 1910.

One such hunting experience he related to me illustrates "the feed the family" point. The weather was very cold and the Brazos river back-water had iced over. On a goose hunt he located a flock of geese holding tightly together as they swam in a small unfrozen area in the ice.

Under cover he closed the distance and took a shot with his 10 Gauge shotgun at the geese while they were sitting on the water at a distance of about 20 yards. He recalled that he killed 17 geese before they could fly away; enough meat for canning and many delicious meals that winter.

His weapon was the Model 87, 10 Gauge Winchester Lever Action produced from 1887 to 1898. It wasn't until the early 1900's that individual states began to pass laws to protect game birds from total extinction. The passage of these laws came from the urging of the concerned sports hunter and their associations who pushed the state legislatures to pass game conservation laws.

Chapter 4 - Some Bad Shooting

My parents gave me my first firearm on my 13th birthday. It was a .410 single shot break down style for 2-1/2" shells rather than a bolt action. Mostly I hunted squirrels but I do remember killing quite a few doves. My style was to jump shoot them out of goat weeds. When they flew straight away I was usually fairly successful, but when they flew laterally I mostly missed the dove, not knowing really how much to LEAD. Later on, after I reached age 15, I acquired a used bolt action .22 Caliber rifle, clip fed. We lived in a sparsely populated rural area.

Hunting and shooting became my passion and I could do it almost anywhere without endangering anyone. I perfected the ability to hit objects thrown into the air with shots from my .22 Rifle. This took many boxes of .22 short ammo and a summer of practice but I became quite good at this skill. In my best days I could hit a twenty-five cent piece thrown into the air if it remained within 20 feet of my position eight out of ten attempts. Now be reminded that I did not use twenty-five cent pieces for practice. I did use caps from bottled drinks. However, this skill with the rifle did not seem to carryover very effectively into my wing-shooting with a shotgun.

When I was age 16 my uncle had a 12 gauge double barrel with "ear" hammers that he allowed me to use. IT did need repairs for I remember the screw for the right hammer had been lost but the hammer fit tightly enough to allow hunting. To avoid losing the hammer it was tied to the gun with a short string. I recall one frustrating occasion hunting with the double.

A friend and I had acquired a box of shot-shells and went to a farming area where I had seen large flights containing hundreds of doves. We "setup" on a grain field where there were a great number of doves feeding. I was stationed under a tree along the eastern edge of the field with the sun at my back and on what we judged to be the flyway. My friend set out to circle the field to jump doves hoping they would fly around the edge of the field and circle by me for we had but one gun and it was MY Uncle's.

My friend was very successful and I had plenty of shooting as the doves flew by me laterally at about 30 yards within easy range at a speed of (as I look back in memory) about 40 mph. I tried LEADs all the way up to three feet. By the time my friend had circled the field; I had shot all 25 rounds of our one box of field load shells and had not hit one dove. Not a feather flew. I simply did not have a clue as to how much LEAD to allow in that wing-shooting situation.

Since then I have continued to hunt waterfowl and upland birds. In the years following the dove missing experience I had other wing shot misses and I can still distinctly remember many of them. Most (but not all) of the "good shot" kills all fade in recall but the scenes that describe the dreaded misses are still vividly etched in my memory as if they occurred only yesterday.

One winter in the early 1970's a friend named Harry Fido and I were in a goose pit near the town of Ware, Illinois, watching the hundreds of Canada Geese work our grain field. With our calls we worked one gaggle of about 30 Canada geese as they took interest in our decoys and circled us. They then came in directly into the north wind and directly toward our decoys and to our blind broadside. A more beautiful sight could not exist.

I still see them in my memories' eye approaching our decoys at about 20 feet elevation, talking to one another about what it was they were going to do. As they approached us with locked wings, heads down at a range of about 25 yards Harry and I began shooting and emptied our chambers and magazines at those huge Canada geese as they gained altitude directly over our heads and guess what; we got nary a one. Woe. What a disappointing result. Neither of us was able to convince the other what we had done incorrectly. We did get our limit of two geese each later that day, but I'll never forget those perfectly decoying beautiful Canada geese we missed so cleanly. Did I LEAD them too much or too little? I had not a clue!

On another occasion in about the same time frame in my hunting life I was hunting Lake Carlisle, a reservoir in Southern Illinois about 60 miles east of St. Louis, Missouri. The weather was an early morning "very cool blue sky" nice. With my decoys set up west of my cover on a beautiful stretch of water, the sun to my back, a flock of about 20 mallards responded to my calling and took a turn to the east into a rising sun toward my decoys and came straight in.

What I remember was mostly Greenheads with their beautiful iridescent colors glistening in the early morning sun as they flew closer and closer. I could taste baked mallard as they approached directly at my cover in such a beautiful "wing set" formation. At about 20 yards my Winchester 12 gauge side-by-side barked twice and the mallards flared, turned tail and were soon out of range. Again we got no birds. How in the world could I miss? They were almost flying down my gun barrels.

Did I LEAD too much or too little? Straight in was a hard shot for me, it seemed.

On missing quail I have found one of the hardest shots for me is attempting to take a flushed quail that rises high and then flies away in a descending flight path. I find them extremely hard to hit because I apparently instinctively shoot over a bird in such a flight pattern. In such cases, where the flight is straight away I have come to believe the problem is concentration to take my LEAD under the descending bird. I have to really work at getting the sight picture right rather than just shooting at them in general. Some instructors warn of such temptations and advise the hunter to focus on a specific feature of the bird, such as the head, or eye or beak. This technique must be developed over time by the individual shooter, depending on one's keenness of eyesight.

The larger the bird the larger, the larger feature will be to focus on. On small birds, like quail, if I can get the head in focus I am doing well. For all the fun I have had hunting quail, they also have given me countless frustrating opportunities during which, too often, I have failed to connect. These are the memories that keep me going back to the field in pursuit of quail.

Chapter 5 - Some Good Shooting

Happily, all my shooting experiences have not been misses so I do not want to sound like a poor loser. Let me share a few successes to balance my account. One occasion was with Rio Bravo Outfitters, out of Brackettville, Texas, located in upper South Texas 30 miles east of Del Rio. This quail hunt was in a very good year and the quail population was at a peak. Three of us came upon a feeding area where a very large covey of Blue Scaled Quail and an equally large covey of Bob Whites all ran into some adjacent heavy cactus cover; an absolutely dreamed about situation; an estimated 50 to 60 birds in heavy cover. As Blues are prone to do, they led in the running and the entire population of quail spread among the cactus.

We determined that there was some open space and if spread out and made our way slowly we could manage the cactus. Walking fast through cactus is not recommended. In my own case, in about the next 15 minutes, I bagged my limit of 15 birds from that congregation as doubles and singles flushed for me within easy gun range. And I did miss a few, but got a couple doubles to make up for the misses.

Way back, during my college years I fondly remember (in detail) having a very successful duck shoot with Granddad's 10 Gauge lever action shotgun. Yes, the very one that took all those geese in Granddad's younger day's. This was a fun hunt involving, for me, a fantastic experience with wing shooting. In late January, 1949, I was on semester break from North Texas Agriculture College in Arlington, Texas.

With this free time I went to visit my grandparents about 90 miles west in Parker County, near the small village of Dennis, Texas, and to do a little hunting while there. It was very cold that week and a snow and ice storm had frozen my grandparents, literally, into their farmhouse because at their age they could not safely manage ice underfoot. The aftermath of the ice was enough to stop all rural traffic, thus unable to hitch-hike the last mile or so, I walked to their home on their 72 acre farm.

It was surprise visit and needless to say they were delighted to see one of their five grandchildren; all boys. On arriving I found ice heaped on the steps leading into the house and they low on drinking water. I soon had water drawn, again literally with rope and bucket, from the well some distance from the house and after I had taken care of a few chores we visited all afternoon.

The next morning early, looking to help with the menu, I took the lever action 10 Gauge and set off on a game hunt. Any edible game would do. It was bitter cold and I did not expect to see even a squirrel out of it's' nest. I had not gone but perhaps 100 yards from the farm-house when I heard something much unexpected. For in all my hunts on and around Granddad's farm I had never even seen a duck. But I heard ducks chattering; and not far away. After a sneak I found several Mallards in a small open water area in the frozen backwater of Kickapoo Creek, a tributary of the Brazos.

The ducks were a good 15 feet down an embankment below my level and my cover was wrong to get a good shot. To correct this I quietly and quickly backed off and circled around to come up on the ducks from the west. After getting in position I flushed them. In so doing the Mallards jumped and took a flight path up passing near me, and then straight away from my position. As they came up out of the creek climbing for altitude in single file I took three of them in as many shots. They all fell on the opposite bank in an area easy to retrieve from and that morning I set my heart on having a just such a 10 Gauge one day.

By the 1950's, even in rural America, shot-gunning for fowl had long been transformed into the fine sport of wing shooting. And I had become a part of it. I will detail for you how Grandmother prepared those three mallards for a "lip-smackin', finger-licking good" meal for I still remember that part too. Oh, if you insist I will give you the yummy details. She boiled water, put it in a bucket and plunged those Mallards one at a time into the hot water. The feathers just slid off. She then held each bird over the open flame to singe the feather fuss off the birds. Thus prepared, she then de-breasted each duck, separating the thighs and legs. Each breast was then "pounded" into tender submission with an appropriate tool built for such meat tenderizing procedures.

Next, she took the tenderized meat and placed it into a saline bath for an hour or so. After this she applied appropriate amounts of flour, salt and pepper and placed the portions into hot lard. In a few minutes, careful not to over cook, she had the neatest pile of tender chicken-fried mallard duck you would ever want to see. Cream gravy was quickly made to go with the hot biscuits and you know the rest. Now see what you have done making me tell you this story. I am hungry for such a feed.

Aren't you also?

Chapter 6 - Wing Shooting Frustration

Wing shooting can be a lot of fun. If you can hit the flying target! Pheasant, Chucker, Woodcock, Grouse, Quail, and Dove, Duck and Geese along with others commonly hunted today. All offer great field shooting enjoyment and fine eating for the wing shooter. As one can imagine each of these species presents unique shooting challenges to the hunter. Some of the faster flying species seem to challenge the shooter by offering seemingly impossible to hit fast moving targets.

Let me admit that this book on "Wing Shooting LEAD" is not going to help those Woodcock or Ruffed Grouse hunters who get their brief shooting opportunities in woods and brush, as much as it can help those who shoot the wide open spaces of most waterfowl, Prairie Pheasant or Quail and Dove.

Oh, I have taken my share of wing shots at quail in heavy cover. Snap shooting is all I can call it. If your instincts are finely tuned you may even be able to build in some LEAD in these brief glimpses at the birds as they expertly put wood between you and them.

Frustration! can remember Green-wing and Blue-wing Teal zipping by my blind at about 60 miles per hour (mph) out at 40 yards. This was in the days of lead shot when 40 yards was a good bet. As a young hunter I shot many rounds at teal in such situations and mostly the birds simply waved their tail feathers goodbye. There they go, gaining altitude into the sunrise and out of sight. And I would be LEADING them a good six feet with my lead 6's in a high velocity shell. Surely that was enough! What happened? Was my six foot LEAD on that teal too much? Or did I LEAD him too little? (We'll see later!)

On all these occasions I thought to myself, "If I had known for certain what LEAD would have been even close to the correct amount I would have been happy indeed."

Chapter 7 - The LEAD Methods

7.1 Help from Friends

In my experience the troubled wing shooter is often instructed by shooting friends on what corrective measures should be tried to establish a better aim. These help sessions bring little if any success. Although with repeated outings the shooter gains in skill in handling the shotgun, many shooters with all the help they can get still have no idea how much to LEAD the target. One person says "this much" another says "that much." One person says "This way" and another says "That way." Often, in such situations many details on how to LEAD are offered.

But, "How much LEAD?" invariable remains the unanswered question of the day in the lives of many wing shooters; "Am I holding too much LEAD, or too little?" Even though many articles have been written instructing anxious readers with sage advice on wing shooting they do not seem to help much. These articles are well written and read with interest but unfortunately the question of "HOW MUCH LEAD?" has still not been effectively answered.

7.2 The "Swing Through" Method

This is likely the most successfully used technique and many authors have instructed on how to use the "swing through" method. These authors seldom, however, tell you how much to LEAD. Here the shooter is advised to start the gun pointing behind the bird and smoothly swing through the bird and when the point of aim is just so you can see "daylight" past the bird's bill or beak to squeeze the trigger; and to continue to follow through with your swing.

This "follow-through" gives the shot time to leave your gun before you "freeze the gun in position" allowing the bird to fly on "out of position." Also to some degree the swing will give the shot pellet pattern a more elongated shape in the bird's line-of-flight. This "keep the gun moving" is excellent advice, and works wonderfully for most anyone on close in slow flying birds. By "slow flying" I mean up to 20 miles per hour and by "close in" I mean inside 20 yards. If the amount of "daylight" you provide (LEAD) is not too much or too little past the bird's nose. Beyond these "close-in" shot situations one really needs to know something of the IDEAL LEAD requirement. I admit that accomplished wing shooters can get birds most of the time using this method. What they unconsciously do, I have been told by them, is to vary the speed of the gun muzzle in it's arc and the amount of "daylight" they allow as they swing past the flying bird. And all this is done depending heavily on their instinctive knowledge of the bird's speed and distance.

Let me give an example. A few years ago I was privileged to participate in a bird hunt on Olin Corporation's Nilo Farm above Alton, Illinois. (At that time Olin manufactured powder and loaded ammo in their Alton Works.)

At one point in the all day hunt we were pass-shooting Pen Raised Mallards at tree top level. The blinds were set up in a shallow swale so grade was 10 feet or so lower than the base of the adjoining trees. The mallards were routed over us on their way to a pond to the north. As they passed over they were doing close to 60 miles per hour on a "downhill" flight path and were a good 100 feet up. We were having trouble hitting them. Take this quick quiz. What LEAD then would you hold on these mallards under the above circumstances?

This was in the days before steel shot so we were shooting lead #6's in Field Loads. Look at the LEAD-O-TABLE on Page 96, under the 30 and 35 yard columns and read the IDEAL LEAD off the row opposite 60 miles per hour. One can see the IDEAL LEAD was between nine and ten feet. Holding a swing through method just past the duck's bill on these fast moving mallards would leave you missing them completely as you shot some eight to nine feet behind them. It was after a quick mental calculation that I determined that my LEAD needed to be nearer 10 feet. I was soon getting my share of the mallards. I used the "Swing Through Method" with follow through and triggered my shots at around 10 feet in front of the mallard.

So as this experience illustrates quite well, if the bird is doing 60 mph and out at 35 yards or beyond, the swing through method needs some help. The help it needs is "how far past the bird's bill or beak do I pull the trigger?"

7.3 The "LEAD and Hold" Method.

This method again presumes you know how much to LEAD. You bring your aim to bear in front of the bird the amount of your chosen LEAD and hold this lead as you pull the trigger. But if you miss, we all will some of the time, you still have the same old question. Did I LEAD too much or too little?

On a hunt sometime ago as we were shooting quail in singles after a flush and in the rush to get off my shots was pulling the trigger before I had my aim properly held. In other words I was shooting (low brass 7-1/2 pellets) well behind the birds with both shots from my over and under 12 gauge.

I promised myself that in order to correct this I was going to say the words "I am LEADING you," as I took my shots at the next single that we flushed. In just a moment then we did flush a single and it was on my side and flying lateral to me so as promised I took my time and said "I am LEADING you," aloud while using the swing through method on the bird (20 yards out at 40 mph) and shot behind him twice.

As he sailed away I realized I had overlooked that my LEAD needed to be about four feet and had again triggered my shots with insufficient LEAD.

7.4 The "Bird Length" Method

There has been some research done to determine appropriate LEAD using "bird lengths" as the unit of measure. Being aware of LEAD in terms of bird lengths and using that measure to sharpen your wing shooting skills can be effective for the wing shooter who has frequent exposure to certain shooting situations that tend to be repetitive.

I am more of an occasional wing shooter. Perhaps I will bird hunt four to five times over a three-month period in the fall of the year. So my efforts at using: "bird lengths" have not been too successful.

7.5 The "Snap Shot" Method

If I instinctively belong in any of these classifications I would put myself down as a "snap-shooter." I want to be a "swing through shooter" and I have to work at not being a "snap shooter." My natural way is simply, by instinct, to estimate the LEAD while aiming the gun and "pow," take my shot. Often even without a simple "follow through." I have heard of some shooters who are able to do remarkably well snap shooting. I am not one of them. Snap shooting quail on the rise with an "open bore" sounds reasonable and easy. It is not easy, for you have to be incredibly fast in reaction time.

Incidentally true "wing shooters" tell me they would not think of snap shooting a rising covey dense with birds rather than at a single bird. They believe it begs "sportsmanship" to do so. I agree such is truly not wing shooting in my classification but is back to the meat hunting of many of our ancestors.

In overview I have not done as well as I would like using any of the methods because I do not shoot enough I guess, or my hand-eye coordination is impaired. After about two days of quail hunting, I begin to become accustom to the emotion of the moment as I experience that exciting feeling during the explosive flushing of a quail covey. It helps when occasionally one can see the quail in the cover before they flush.

Inevitably after two days of hunting I begin to feel sure, were we to hunt another two or three days I would really get to be an excellent wing shot! But I have never hunted quail long enough for this to happen. Two and one-half days has been my longest quail hunt outing.

7.6 Becoming a Passable Shot

But with all the above having been said, I did get to be a "passable" wing-shot after I invented the LEAD-0-TABLE. At least I knew in approximate terms what an appropriate LEAD would be. By "passable," I mean I can take about 60 to 70% of the birds I shoot at. I realize this does not classify me as an expert wing-shooter but in my younger days I have broken 25 trap clays in sequence in competitive shooting a few times.

But, I have to admit, wing shooting in two situations, even by using the "Lead Tables" and knowing the LEAD hasn't helped me very much. These are when the bird is approaching straight in. Somehow I suppose I shoot over the birds. Or while flying straight away while rising or falling in elevation above the ground or water. These shots are frustrating to miss because you know you should have had a hit. Those birds flying straight at you are also hard to practice for. Trap or skeet fields do not typically offer "straight at you" shots, although skeet comes close, but at short range.

7.8 – Real Help Finally Comes

The sense of accomplishment in cleanly and solidly hitting a flying bird provides the shooter with fun and incentive to shoot more frequently. But all too often prospective serious wing-shooters are frustrated by their inability to hit the moving object they are shooting at and this results in discouragement and an indifference toward shooting. Nothing is more discouraging than the feeling of exasperation and embarrassment that comes with an unsuccessful shot-gun shooting outing.

Thus, if a device could be invented or a table created that provided even something close to the correct LEAD, wouldn't the wing shooters of the world flock ("no pun intended") to the inventor's door wanting a copy of this device?

THE LEAD-O-TABLES WERE DEVELOPED TO PROVIDE THE ANSWER TO THAT QUESTION; "HOW MUCH DO I LEAD?"

Chapter 8 - Origin of the LEAD-O-TABLE

In the 1970's I was working in my trade as a mechanical engineer and seriously taking to wing shooting, mainly waterfowl and doves. And I was missing those seemingly easy shots. I recalled that in my university studies there was a law of physics that allowed a person to calculate things like how much LEAD would be required for a moving object to intersect another moving object if at least three of the variables were known.

In the case of wing shooting, I knew that the only variable known with reasonable accuracy was the muzzle velocity of the discharged shot-shell pellets. The distance to the bird was not so much unknown as it was useless and the bird's speed fell in the same category. And as far as I was concerned the appropriate LEAD was unknown as well.

In my practice of engineering I found that manufacturers often designed slide-rules to assist their clients in using the product. It was then I determined that I could build a slide rule that would calculate LEAD. If I could estimate bird speed and distance to the bird and since the shot pellet muzzle velocity was known, armed with these three variables I could calculate a LEAD that would be at least close to that needed to hit a flying object with shot from my shotgun. In a few weeks I did construct such a slide rule, and crude though it was it did allow me to estimate an approximate LEAD for different shooting situations. This was a "lightning bolt from the blue." Now I had more information than I had ever had before. And when I checked the slide-rule it gave me astounding information which when applied in the field actually worked.

The surprising thing was the LEAD calculated using the slide rule, typically turned out to be a lot more than I had thought necessary before. For instance in the example given above page 20-21 where I was shooting doves as they circled the field as my friend spooked them. I was holding a lead from two to three feet. Using my LEAD calculating slide-rule I found I should have been using a LEAD of at least six feet, not my three feet with which I recorded the 25 misses in a row.

See LEAD-O-TABLE on Page 97, for 7-1/2 pellets, 1130 fps, opposite 40 MPH and in the 30 Yards Column.

And at least some of the Teal I spoke of earlier (page 31) would have been in my game bag if I had again almost doubled my LEAD to 11 feet! See LEAD-O-TABLE FOR lead 6's, 1330 fps, on Page 108, opposite 60 MPH and in the 40 Yards column. Wow! Eleven feet is a lot of LEAD. Needless to say, I was at once an astounded and happy hunter. Perhaps, at last, I could do a better job in my wing-shooting. And I did.

Later, after computers came along, I simply used spread-sheet software to make tables to show the required LEAD. I call them the LEAD-O-TABLE.

Chapter 9 - The LEAD-O-TABLE Theory

The LEAD-O-TABLE is a tool based on simple calculations using the Laws of Physics. The answers from such calculations can be used by shooters to determine the approximate LEAD required in wing shooting. I call the calculated LEAD the "IDEAL LEAD." IDEAL because it really represents a close approximation that, while not extremely precise, is at least very close to the required EXACT LEAD. Remember if we can get within a few inches of the EXACT LEAD the shot pattern will take care of the rest.

The LEAD-O-TABLE is based on the mathematical relationship between two moving objects whose paths of travel are to intersect at a point and to which point the objects must arrive simultaneously. As in "shot pellets and a flying target." If this "simultaneous arrival" is to occur then the we must equate the distance the object travels (LEAD) in a fixed amount of time to the what distance the shot pellets will travel (Shot Velocity) to intercept the object in the exact same amount of time. The Law of Physics governing this relationship may be expressed in the terms of a hunter concerned with their ability to hit a flying object as follows:

The Relationships in the laws of Physics:

"LEAD"   *-is to-*   "Object Speed"
    As

"Distance to Object" *-is to-*   "Shot Velocity"

In formula format it will look as follows -

$$\frac{\text{LEAD}}{\text{Object Speed}} = \frac{\text{Distance to Object}}{\text{Shot Velocity}}$$

In the formula format let me use abbreviations as follows:

Let: LEAD - be   LEAD
        Os - be "Object speed"
        Do - be "Distance to object"
        Sv - be "Shot velocity"

Then:

$$\frac{\text{LEAD}}{\text{Os}} = \frac{\text{Do}}{\text{Sv}}$$

Applying algebraic principals we solve for

LEAD:

Then: $\text{LEAD} = \dfrac{Do \times Os}{Sv}$

Example:

Let's assume at the "instant of pulling your trigger" the scene is a flying Quail angling away at a distance of 30 yards with an estimated speed of 40 miles per hour.

For constants we'll use-
  - 3 feet per yard,
  - 5280 feet per mile,
  - 3600 seconds per hour,
  - 7-1/2 shot field load,
  - 1130 feet per second shot velocity

$$\text{LEAD} = \frac{30 \text{ yards} \times 3 \text{ feet in yard} \times 40 \text{ mph} \times 5280 \text{ ft in mile}}{1130 \text{ feet per second} \times 3600 \text{ seconds in hour}}$$

$$LEAD = \frac{19,008,000}{4,068,000}$$

LEAD = 4.67 feet

This calculated LEAD assumes the shot travels at 1130 feet per second the entire distance to the bird. But we know that shot velocity deteriorates due to air friction or air resistance. Thus the 4.67 feet does not allow for shot slowdown due to air resistance. So if you will refer to the LEAD-O-TABLE on Page 97 for 7-1/2 lead shot you will find opposite 40 MPH and in the 30 yards column a LEAD of six (6.0) feet. The additional LEAD of 1.33 feet (4.67 + 1.33 = 6.0 feet) is what is needed to adjust for the effect of wind resistance slowing the shot velocity.

As you can see, the above formula uses "feet per second," (fps) "yards" and "miles per hour" (MPH). The formula may be altered through the use of such factors that are constant to allow the game speed to be expressed in or "kilometers per hour" and the distance to the object in "meters." The units selected depend on the most usable form that would fit the shooter's experience and knowledge base and native instincts on estimating distances and speed. In the USA the units used are "object speed" in

47

"miles per hour," "distance to the bird" in "yards." "Pellet muzzle velocity" in "feet per second" as published (adjusted for wind resistance and distance to the object) and the "LEAD" in "feet."

Chapter 10 - Other Shooting Variables

As the creator of the LEAD-O-TABLE, I recognize that to be rigorously scientific and absolutely exacting there are a number of additional variables to be considered in an exact LEAD calculation than the ones used in the design of the LEAD-O-TABLE. These were discussed above in **1.0 How Much LEAD? Now You Can Know!**

Examples are wind velocity, wind direction, shot-shell temperature, shot velocity slowdown, the density of the air and yes, even gun barrel length and temperature. We have already accounted for shot velocity, bird distance and speed.

Of all these, there are only two additional critical variables that need to be considered by the serious wing shooter. These are pellet "slowdown" (technically termed "velocity deterioration") and the wind conditions. But before we deal with pellet slowdown lets deal again with "Shot Velocity."

10.1 Shot Pellet Velocity

Shot pellet velocity as it exits the muzzle of the gun is primarily dependent on shot-shell design characteristics of powder type and ounces of pellet charge. Pellet velocities generally range from around 1100 to 1500 feet per second with a few reporting 1550.

We know that powder type, powder volume, total shot weight, gun-barrel length and primer type, all affect the muzzle velocity of the pellets. But to get into all these details is not a productive use of time for the average shooter who wants to use the LEAD-O-TABLEs. The only shot-shell information the shooter needs to know to determine LEAD from the LEAD-O-TABLEs is the pellet size and muzzle velocity as it exits the barrel in the manufacturer's test reports.

This measurement is usually taken up to three feet from the muzzle. Some measure the velocity of the first pellet; others measure the average velocity of the entire load. Good velocity information is readily available from a publication by Lyman called the "Shot-shell Handbook" or from manufacturer's sales brochures and is the type of information I have in used in setting up the LEAD-O-TABLEs.

Sure, there is a slight difference from manufacturer to manufacturer in powder, primer and shell case, and from gun to gun because of action and barrel length. But these differences are all of no importance in your quest to determine approximate LEAD from the LEAD-O-TABLEs. All we need is the pellet muzzle velocity and our friend the "pellet pattern" takes care of all these little details as we seek the answer to "How much do I LEAD."

I have seen no LEAD information in any shot-shell information published by manufacturers. It is my firm belief that every wing-shooter deserves at least an approximation of what LEAD to hold in different shooting situations. That approximation is what "WING SHOOTING LEAD" gives you in the LEAD-O-TABLE. While it is not rigorously exact, but only an approximation, it is far better than nothing, which is what has largely been the product of the industry for 200 years and more. So take the LEAD-O-TABLE result and begin your own experiments to improve your kill ratio in the field.

In designing the LEAD-O-TABLEs my approach has been to take ballistics information for three types of shot-shell loads; Field Loads (low brass), Magnum Loads (high brass) and High Velocity loads (also high brass) and construct the LEAD-O-TABLEs for these readily available loads. Dove and quail are usually hunted with Field Loads with 1-1/8 oz shot and 3-1/4 dram equivalent of powder. Muzzle velocity on these loads range around 1100 to 1150 feet per second. Some may hunt dove and quail with high velocity loads but these are the exception rather than the rule.

Waterfowl are usually hunted using Magnum or High Velocity loads. What I have done in order to simplify is to place bird hunter shot shells into three categories of velocity. Field loads, Magnum loads and High Velocity loads (2-3/4", 3" or 3-1/2"). There are LEAD-O-TABLEs for these three different shell families in lead pellets. I also provide six tables for steel shot, two at 1260 feet per second, two at 1370 feet per second and one each at 1450 and 1550 feet per second muzzle velocity for high flying ducks and geese.

Hand-loaders can use whichever table fits or is nearest to the velocity they are loading. To use one that is near is far better than none at all! You can even adjust the LEADs slightly yourself to closer match your load velocity.

10.2 Air Resistance and Pellet Slowdown

As is done in some laboratory experiments, were we to do our shooting in a vacuum where no air resistance existed then the required LEAD would be somewhat easier to calculate.

But, recognizing that pellet velocity deteriorates with distance traveled due to air resistance, this effect was built into the formula shown above as I calculated the values for the LEAD-O-TABLEs. The Laws of Physics say that wind resistance varies with the square of the velocity. The wind resistance at a velocity of 1200 feet per second is four times that at 600 feet per second.

This simply means that the pellet velocity slowdown is not a linear function but one that varies as the square of the velocity. As the shot travels from the gun muzzle the shot velocity reduction in feet per second due to wind resistance is less and less because the pellet velocity is also decreasing. The LEAD-O-TABLE "LEAD" is appropriately adjusted to allow for this pellet velocity deterioration. The calculations for the LEAD-O-TABLEs allow correctly for the LEAD to increase as the distance increases and the pellet velocity decreases. And in the development of the LEAD-O-TABLEs, I tried it both ways, linearly and velocity squared. The difference found between the two methods is not so much at short yardage's but becomes very important as the mid to outer kill range of the shot pellet is reached.

To be even more accurate the LEAD-O-TABLEs in this book have been prepared by taking the typical lapsed "time in seconds" the shot takes to arrive at 20, 40, and 60 yards with different size pellets and muzzle velocities. The LEAD-O-TABLEs are calculated on the basis of this measured lapsed time. This is done by taking the measured time lapse for the pellets to arrive 20, 40 and 60 yards and then calculating by interpolation the velocity deterioration in 5-yard increments beginning with the muzzle velocity as it exits the gun.

Another Law of Physics that effects LEAD is the Law of Gravity. It does not affect the LEAD greatly but let's explore why. The LEAD-O-TABLEs are calculated assuming the shooter is firing at a bird in a roughly horizontal plain. We must recognize that as the angle of the gun barrel relative to the horizon increases with the shooter taking aim at the overhead flying bird the greater the effect of gravity on pellet slowdown. Gravity acts in addition to the wind drag mentioned above. The "Force of Gravity" in physical terms effects pellet velocity at the rate of "32.2 feet per second/per second."

This means that pellets discharged vertically in a vacuum (no wind resistance) would slow down as the rate of 32.2 feet per second for each second after the gun is discharged. The net effect of gravity over the effective range of the shot is not great but is acknowledged. Think about it. At say a 1150 feet per second muzzle velocity and less than a second to the outer limits of the effective killing range, the 32.2 feet per second loss in pellet velocity is less than 5% of the loss due to wind resistance.

Just know this. The LEAD shown in the LEAD-O-TABLE becomes the very minimum LEAD as the angle of the gun barrel is raised above the horizontal. Because the force of gravity effects the discharged shot, hence the LEAD, more as the shot is discharged vertically. But once again the scatter of the pellets becomes the hunter's good friend.

At the shorter overhead ranges the force of gravity on the shot pellets does not have enough time to seriously affect the LEAD. To compensate for gravity when shooting at birds near the outer limits of the effective range of the pellets when shooting vertically overhead the concerned shooter simply adds a little to the IDEAL LEAD.

"How much do I add," you ask. A few inches at the most. In most cases not really enough to worry about.

10.3 The Pellet Drop Variable

Here again we are considering The Force of Gravity, which causes shot pellets fired in the roughly horizontal plane to have dropped at the outer edge of their effective range from up to seven to twelve inches. How many shooters allow for this variable? Few, if any! Why? Because the shot pellet pattern at these distances has a large enough scatter to erase the need to worry about pellet drop.

As I have stated earlier, the same is true in many of the other strict physical considerations in the area of calculating an EXACT target LEAD. The total affect of these variables are lost in the shot pellet pattern at target distances. Were we working with a single rifle bullet these variables would be extremely important and each would have to be considered on its own merit. But, the shot pellet pattern at range is our good friend in the shotgun world of wing shooting.

10.4 Wind Direction Considerations

Shooters should give consideration to the wind when the velocity exceeds five to seven miles per hour. High wind velocities (20 to 40 miles per hour) offer some unique challenges. Remember this rule of thumb; your "shot pellets in the wind" are effected the same way as your target "bird in the wind;" both are airborne and the forces of wind are being applied to both. It is not a direct relationship since the bird's shape, though aerodynamic, is not affected the same as that of round pellets. Birds are of course much larger and as such project a sizable bodily cross section for the wind force to act upon.

The biggest challenge for shooting in windy conditions is overcoming the common tendency shooters have to over adjust (downward) their LEAD for birds flying into the wind since their speed seems so much slower relative to the ground. In fact when birds are flying into a high velocity wind, the shooter must first estimate the wind speed and then the ground speed of the bird and add the two to get the correct speed to use on the LEAD-O-TABLE. Again at short ranges this can be ignored but at 30 to 60 yards wind velocity does become a deciding factor in determining correct LEAD.

In many situations, shooting as if there were no wind will prove satisfactory. But remember, the wind is also affecting the shot pellet, so to LEAD less for the apparently slower flying bird will often result in shooting behind the target, especially at long ranges.

Lets face it, the wind does complicate things some, but why should we not know from the LEAD-O-TABLE what the IDEAL LEAD should be were there no wind. At least you have something to work with as you adjust your LEAD for the wind conditions. It is better to take the IDEAL LEAD information provided by the LEAD-O-TABLE and work with it thus allowing you to adapt more quickly to the windy conditions. A close approximation as to the LEAD required is vastly better than being without any knowledge at all.

10.5 Angle of Flight and Taking your LEAD

The possible configurations (angle) of bird flight in relation to your position as shooter are infinite. After you have determined your approximate LEAD from the LEAD-O-TABLES you have one more factor to keep in mind. The LEAD you hold on the bird must always be estimated "in-line-of-flight" of the bird. It is really quite simple. As the bird is flying just remember the LEAD you have chosen must be held in front of the bird in the direction the bird is flying. I call this "in-line-of-flight."

For instance, say the bird is flying quartering away from you. Your task is to hold the LEAD so as to discharge the shotgun so the shot pellets intercept the bird at the position the bird is going to be "in-line-of-flight" a split second later. The bird is going to be further along the path it is now flying. Hence aim "in-line-of-flight." All this is true unless you are shooting doves that have seen a lot of hunting pressure. In this case, your guess is better than mine as to which direction the dove is going to "jink" just as you pull the trigger. I haven't yet invented a "jink" detector so good shooting!

Another point I wish to make is that there are numerous situations in wing shooting, especially waterfowl, that one simply takes very little LEAD, if any. Why? Because the bird you are shooting for is in such a flight angle that the result after applying the LEAD "in line of flight" is you need only to shoot directly at the bird. What are some of these? For instance, if the bird is descending directly at you from overhead, or conversely, rising directly away from you in a flight path that in taking your LEAD "in-line-of-flight" you still simply shoot directly at the bird. While these shots are not necessarily easy, in these cases you do not need a LEAD-O-TABLE to decide what you need to do.

In such situations, one simply makes a quick observation and allows for any minor lateral movement and fires away. Other "little if any LEAD needed" situations are in taking a waterfowl as they take off from the water. Their speed of flight is low as they become airborne and the LEAD requirement is often negligible. Or, just after they lower their webs to make a water landing and their speed has become very slow. These "low lateral movement" flight situations are wonderful opportunities to score kills by using any of the "LEAD methods."

For instance, pheasant often rise vertically for several feet before moving laterally. In such a configuration, if your reflexes are fast enough, you can take them with little if any LEAD. Other upland birds occasionally give one similar easy targets.

But the LEAD-O-TABLE becomes a powerhouse of information for those frequently occurring situations where the flight configuration (angle) is repetitive and significant LEAD is required, as in pass shooting doves or ducks and geese. If a shooter is missing most of their shots, discouragement sets in and they begin to wonder just what am I doing wrong? Or in a duck blind the where the birds are presenting repetitive pass shooting opportunities and misses are frequent we find discouragement sets in. It is in these situations that the usefulness of the LEAD-O-TABLE becomes more apparent and exhibits its utility as it gives those long sought after answers to the 200 year-old question of "How much should I LEAD?"

10.6 Barrel Chokes and Your LEAD

Shotgun barrel chokes affect the amount of pellet spread as your pellets gain distance from the gun muzzle. Chokes are effective and are recommended but chokes do not effect the required LEAD; shot pellet pattern does, however. The full choke barrel does not give the shooter the latitude in aiming as does the improved cylinder. Thus the less spread of the shot pattern the more critical the LEAD.

But, chokes are very critical in determining effective range of pellets because the pellet pattern is affected. And the pellet pattern affects your ability to get numbers of pellets into a given circle at a given distance. The effective killing range of the pellet is determined by the mass of the pellet. Larger (heavier) pellets kill at longer ranges than smaller pellets. Understanding this relationship between shot pellet type, velocity and the pellet weight's effect on killing range is very important. I recommend that you use the proper choke for the bird, the habitat in which you are hunting and the shooting situation.

Choke Spread in feet - Typical	20 yards	30 yards	40 yards	50 yards	60 yards
Full Choke	1.3	2.2	3.3	5.0	
Modified	1.7	2.8	3.8	5.5	
Improved Cylinder	2.2	3.2	4.3		
Cylinder Bore	2.7	3.7	4.9		

This table by omission of data suggests the effective killing ranges of shotguns and chokes.

Chapter 11 - Give Up or FIGHT?

Over the years some of the more exacting shooters have concluded that since we cannot ever calculate the exact lead why bother? Given the high tech lasers and other targeting technology available today one could be sure that given enough money an electronic device could be developed to take all the talent out of shooting airborne objects with shotguns. If this were done then we really would have lost the activity as a sport.

The basic question comes to this. Why let the confusion that comes with all the variables deny the shooter the knowledge of what the approximate LEAD should be in ideal conditions? With the approximate LEAD in mind the shooter faced, for instance, with a windy day can know better how to allow for the wind velocity.

So, we can adopt a fatalistic attitude and "give up" or we can take the IDEAL LEAD information provided by the LEAD-O-TABLE and adapt more quickly to the conditions of the day. A close approximation of the LEAD required is vastly better than being without any knowledge at all. I call it "fight."

Knowing the IDEAL LEAD will help even the novice shooter in getting more game. But even with an idea as to the correct LEAD, practice still is going to be needed if you are to become a reasonably good wing shot. I recall hunting pheasant in Illinois near the town of Pontiac, in the 1970's. Frequently I would hunt with a friend who worked for Olin, the maker of ammunition.

The typical field scenario was that we would be walking along through the cover when a cock pheasant would suddenly come "busting" out of the corn and "boom" down it would go. Quick like, the bird was in the bag before I could even bring my shotgun to bear on it. I soon realized that my reflexes needed a lot of help.

On inquiry, he told me that he did a lot of trap and skeet shooting at the Olin range. Soon I joined a trap team and my skills improved markedly. Nothing is better than trap or skeet to hone those wing-shooting reflexes.

What am I saying? I am saying even if you can approximate the correct LEAD, having the reflex part down will often be the difference between a successful hunt and coming home with no birds. As in any sport practice makes perfect; if not perfect then at least passable. To shoot at this level of expertise requires practice, practice, practice. This will sharpen your reaction time and improve your accuracy.

Think about it. If we are not tuned up, then when that opportunity comes; a quail flushes and we in a great hurry will often shoot before we really aim and that shot will miss, then in desperation we shoot again and it too is too little too late. If we are shooting an automatic we finally get the aim right, the sight picture just right and the LEAD perfect but alas the bird is too far a way to kill.

At least that is how I do it if I do not practice.

Chapter 12 - Estimating the Flying Speeds of Birds

Doing research on bird flying speeds has not been easy. Some information has been gathered from experience and some from reading what others have recorded about typical flying speeds.

While driving an automobile along a paved road I have clocked doves at 45 miles per hour while the bird was obviously in a relaxed "cruising" mode. When they turn on the after burners I read where they can attain speeds of 60 mph or more. Me, I believe I have seen diving doves doing over 70 mph when really frightened and also "jinking" as they go.

Ducks and geese in full flight have been reported to easily sustain speeds between 50 and 60 mph. Some have reported canvasbacks at speeds over 75 mph. Teal are very fast on the wing; again I read where speeds of 60 mph have been recorded. Geese can "zip" just like the faster ducks also, though as a larger bird they look like they are flying slower than they are. It is easy to under estimate the flying speed of a goose.

Quail fly away from a flush at speeds of up to 40 to 50 mph. Chucker and Grouse about the same but in the field in most situations all tend to the slower speeds of 40 mph. Pheasant can fly up to 50 to 60 mph when fleeing. So if you can get your reflexes tuned to get them on the rise before they turn horizontal with the afterburners on you will have better luck getting your bird. A pheasant angling away is a hard shot because they are gaining speed as you are aiming.

What I do in the field is to take the above flying speed information and make an attempt in estimating the target bird's speed in miles per hour. With practice most hunters will become sufficiently proficient at estimating speeds and distances to be successful in using the LEAD-O-TABLEs. In my own case, being a football fan, I estimate distances in terms of 5 to 10 yard increments when bird hunting and in 100 yard increments when hunting with a rifle.

To learn to estimate distances one needs to use something in your life that you know the length or width of and use multiples of this to estimate your distances. For instance a large automobile is about five to six yards long. You can even use the width or length of a room in your home or office for your reference standard. As you get set up in a duck blind simply make it your business to know the yardage out to the outer most decoys.

Chapter 13 - Non-Lead & Steel Shot

Since I was unable to find data for bismuth loads I have no charts for bismuth. You can either use the tables for lead or steel since the density is about half way in between lead and steel. Adjust LEAD accordingly; down from lead, up from steel. For instance, LEAD for a duck flying 40 MPH at 40 yards for a # 4 lead field load, 1130 feet per second (fps) muzzle velocity load is 7.9 feet, while that for # 4 steel at 1370 feet per second muzzle velocity will be about 6.4 feet. I have read where the short 2-1/2 inch bismuth shot shells are loaded at about 1250 feet per second (fps) muzzle velocity   souse a chart near this velocity if you wish.

Steel pellets are only 70% of the weight of lead and the steel pellet is more` rigid than a lead pellet. A lead pellet is considered soft when compared to a steel pellet. Thus as the steel shot charge leaves the barrel through the choke it is a more rigid mass (the individual steel pellets are not deformed as much as lead pellets.) Thus shot charges of steel pellets cause more stress in the barrel. So the introduction of steel pellets in shot-shells changed the required gun barrel metallurgy and barrel design require-ments is some shotguns.

Since steel is not as heavy as lead the shot muzzle velocity was increased to compensate (make up for lower mass with higher velocity) and thus the LEAD requirements for steel in bird hunting were decreased. Since steel shot is lighter than lead it (same shot size) has less mass (energy) at game range than lead. As such, steel falls victim to slowdown due to air friction more than lead. Thus, powder loads in steel shot-shells are designed to give the shot a bit more velocity than lead shot.

Shot pellet velocity is determined by the pressure created by the burning powder pushing the shot out of the barrel. Typical lead shot pellets exit the shotgun muzzle at velocities ranging from 1100 to 1400 fps depending on the particular powder load in the shell. A few factory loads may exit at slower velocities and a few at higher velocities. In steel pellets (same size as lead) various, typically higher, shot velocities are being used, from 1250 fps or so to 1375 fps. In 2004 even higher velocity loads of 1450 and 1550 feet per second are available. This additional velocity assists in giving the steel additional energy at range to bag the game. For some shooters it may also give more range. Also the shot-shell suppliers have offered a wider and more readily available selection of larger size pellets in steel in order to provide the energy needed in the individual pellet to successfully take the bird. The introduction of the 3-1/2 inch shot-shell has also helped to give room for a larger total steel pellet count to improve the killing range pattern density.

In general, hunters use "F," "T," and "BB" and "BBB" steel pellet sizes for the larger waterfowl. Some have recommended that the hunter shooting steel choose a pellet size two to three sizes larger than in the lead used before. Such a selection will provide the added mass needed for penetration at game range.

Also shooting steel pellets in guns designed only for lead can be hazardous in certain situations, particularly in older guns. Lead pellets being somewhat moldable exiting the barrel are easier on the barrel, but steel being more rigid can damage a gun barrel not designed for steel pellets. In some cases catastrophic gun damage has been seen which can be hazardous to the health of the shooter and any companions standing nearby. High quality, late model guns "may" handle steel pellets OK, and they may not. It is wise to consult with the gun manufacturer or a knowledgeable gunsmith. In my own case I bought a new gun designed for steel pellets. Not a lot of steel pellet velocity information has been published but I have managed to get enough to provide you with a six LEAD-O-TABLES for steel.

Regarding steel shot, I know experienced hunters who do not advise one to try shots beyond 40 yards. That to do so results in too many wounded birds. That steel is not acceptably effective at greater yardage.

The LEAD-O-TABLES are constructed with 60 miles per hour and 60 yards range as the outer limits. This gives one the knowledge of what is happening to the LEAD as the distance increases. The TABLES are not, by the use of "60 and 60," recommending these distances for probable kills. Smaller shot have shorter kill ranges than do heavier or larger shot. Lead can kill further than bismuth or steel because the heavier shot has greater momentum for penetration.

Chapter 14 - Trap Shooting and LEAD

Trap shooting is an excellent sport in and of itself, and for the wing-shooter of game birds it is an excellent way to sharpen reflexes and improve aim. When a bird flushes it is important to get the gun up and on the target before it flies out of range. Quicker reflexes through trap shooting mean "shots off" at shorter ranges and shorter ranges mean better kill ratios.

With all the instruction I ever had in trap shooting I never even thought to ask; "How fast are those clay pigeons flying when they escape from the launcher? Or "How fast are they going at the "break" range?" I've read books and books on trap shooting and have yet to see clay target velocities discussed.

Shooting form, gun types, shot types and all that but nothing on trap or skeet clay bird velocities are all discussed in books and magazine articles.

But, the big question is: "How many miles per hour is a clay bird traveling right out of the launcher?"

I finally found the answer at a sports-show where a manufacturer of launchers told me that in both skeet and trap the clays leave the launcher between 40 and 45 miles per hour. Much like a quail getting up; but different than a quail for a flushed quail is going to gain speed as it flies away.

Not so a clay bird; it is going to lose velocity as it fights air density. A clay bird would only gain speed if you were shooting trap in a 50 MPH following wind; hardly likely. Clays lose velocity out of the launcher at varying rates depending on vertical angle of launch and the wind speed and direction. If we were to combine only a few variables like wind velocity, flight angle, gun, ammo, shooter experience and post position into scenarios there would be over a hundred possible scenarios in determining an exact LEAD in Trap Shooting.

But just because the sport shooting of clays is complex does not prevent us from considering the simple theoretical elements of LEAD. Since LEAD is a function of distance, target velocity, and pellet velocity lets look at these in the following paragraphs and see some resulting theoretical LEADS for clay targets.

The second question in Trap shooting is, "How far away from the shooter are trap clay birds launched?

Answer; from 16 to 27 yards. Distances greater than 16 yards (17 to 27) are used to handicap the expert shooters. In Trap shooting, targets are usually broken at 30 to 45 yards; a little over 30 for the closer in handicap yardage and nearer 45 yards (perhaps a few yards more in some cases) for the longer handicap yardage.

But, in theory, were you were fast enough to kill a clay bird just as it left the launcher on a 16 yard event, how much LEAD would need to be applied?

Let's pick 20 yards. (I am not saying that this is the best yardage at which to break the clay!) The way to get a very good idea of how much LEAD might be required is to look at the LEAD-O-TABLE for 7-1/2 lead pellets (what I shoot at clays) in a field load because this approximates trap load velocities. If you are loading your own shot-shells simply use the TABLE that matches your velocity and pellet size.

Looking at page 99 - #7-1/2 shot - 1130 fps Muzzle Velocity - Field Load, find 40 mph and 45 mph (range of launch speed) in the vertical column on the left side of the TABLE Then refer to the "Yards to Target" row across the upper part of the chart and find on 20 yards. Next down the 20 Yard column we see the following:

At 40 MPH and 20 Yards we see a LEAD of 3.7 feet.

At 45 MPH and 20 Yards we see a LEAD of 4.2 feet.

So about "four feet LEAD" would be required at 20 yards to kill the bird at that instant. Only in demonstrations of shooting skill have I seen trap broken immediately out of the launcher. The expert that was doing it was near the launcher and shooting his automatic from the hip! And hitting every clay launched. I am not sure a 27-yard handicap is enough for such expert shooters.

What happens next after the launch? The clay bird starts to slow down and to get further away. It slows down at a rate that is proportional to the square of it's velocity. What does "square of the velocity" mean. Simply put it slows down less and less as a percentage of its velocity the further it gets from the shooter. In trap how far does a clay travel from the shooter before it strikes the ground? Depending on the wind and assuming a level surface all the way from the shooter to the landing point of near 50 yards; with substantial wind some a tad further.

Let's quit asking questions and set up a scenario and examine LEADs for -

35 MPH and 30 Yards (all yardage's are from the shooter),
30 MPH and 35 Yards and
20 MPH and 40 Yards
10 MPH and 45 Yards

At 35 MPH and 30 Yards we see a LEAD of 5.2 feet
At 30 MPH and 35 Yards we see A LEAD of 5.4 feet
At 20 MPH and 40 Yards we see a LEAD of 4.3 feet
At 10 MPH and 45 Yards we see a LEAD of 2.5 feet

So in this scenario the LEAD changes over the course of it's flight only slightly more than one foot until it slows and is about to drop to the ground. The appropriate LEAD is around 4.5 to 5.5 feet all the way out to 40 yards.

Let's look at another scenario. Assume a 20 MPH tail wind on the clay. So what happens? The clay is still 40 to 45 MPH out of the launcher but slows down much slower. For instance let's look at the following situations:

At 40 MPH and 30 Yards we see a LEAD of 6.0 feet.
At 35 MPH and 35 Yards we see a LEAD of 6.3
At 30 MPH and 40 Yards we see a LEAD of 6.4 feet.
At 15 MPH and 45 Yards we see a LEAD of 4.2 feet.

Thus the approximate LEAD is about 6 plus feet all the way out to 40 Yards. Then as the velocity deteriorates due to wind effect we see the LEAD drop to around 4 feet. So what has happened? The clay slows down slower sooner requiring more LEAD.

But what about the shot pellets, isn't the wind assisting them a little? A "little" is the right word. Twenty MPH is about 30 fps. The muzzle velocity is 1130 fps. What percentage of the muzzle velocity is 30 fps. It is 2.6%; a little; but, what about the clay? It is leaving the launcher around 66 fps and the wind is 30 fps so the clay is getting a boost from the wind that is 50% of it's' initial velocity. Quite a difference! Oh, the clay is going to slow down all right but at a lot slower rate.

We have looked at scenarios with no wind and with a 20 MPH tailing wind. Let's now look at a 20 MPH headwind. What is going to happen to a clay bird launched into a head-wind? Sometimes they rise rapidly presenting a target higher above the horizon, but every time they will slow down faster. With the launch velocity still 40 to 45 MPH out of the launcher let's look at 30 yards and 30 MPH, 35 Yards and 20

MPH, 40 yards and 15 MPH and 45 yards and 10 MPH.

At 30 MPH and 30 Yards we see a LEAD of 4.5 feet.
At 20 MPH and 35 Yards we see a LEAD of 4.2 feet.
At 15 MPH and 40 Yards we see a LEAD of 4.2 feet.
At 10 MPH and 45 Yards we see a LEAD of 2.5 feet

So the wind makes a BIG difference in LEAD required in trap shooting. LEADs from four to six feet are common.

Looking back at the yardage's used in my illustration one can see I have purposely picked a span of velocities (MPH) and yardage's to illustrate a theoretical scenario. These were selected for illustrative purposes only and will likely not represent the situation when the reader is at the trap field.

What am I saying? Every day is a different day. Weather conditions vary. Guns and ammo vary. Shooters vary. What I do in "Wing Shooting LEAD" is offer to the trap shooter in these paragraphs an insight into what you are facing and what some of the LEADs might be. This insight on LEADs is much more than I ever had and will help the shooter to understand why, in surprise, some targets are broken and more importantly why, also in surprise, some targets are not broken. And understanding why this might be happening to you.

I have prepared the following chart showing one theoretical scenario and how the LEAD required changes as the clay covers the distance from the launcher until it drops.

But do remember this, the shot pellet load as it gains distance from the muzzle is spreading wider and wider. This spread becomes the trap shooters good friend in one way and bad friend in another. Spread is our good friend as we are slightly off of a true LEAD and the spread allows the error and we register a kill. Spread is our bad friend as distance from the gun increases and pattern density decreases.

Thus at longer ranges the pattern density may allow the clay to pass right through your pattern and not have enough pellets strike it to get a kill. So remember with the pattern spreading you will sometimes see kills that are off of what you selected as the TABLE indicated LEAD.

As stated this is because of pattern spread and other variables. But when you "center the clay" with a full load at the closer ranges puts it into thousands of pieces, it is then you know you had very close to the exact LEAD required on that particular clay bird.

I strongly recommend that you take the time to pattern the gun you are using for trap shooting. Pattern it from 20 yards to 50 yards at 5-yard intervals. That will require seven targets for one round at each distance. If you want to become good at trap shooting, knowing how your gun patterns at different distances is vital to your overall knowledge base.

Also remember this. Trap clays are sometimes launched at angles to the shooter. In Positions 1 and 5 the clay is sometimes almost lateral to the left or right; at other times the clay will be near straight away. In taking your LEAD always take it "in-line-of-flight" of the clay. A four-foot LEAD straight away is to shoot directly at the clay while allowing for rise or drop.

Pick your LEAD method ("swing through" - "hold a sustained LEAD" or "snap shoot") and execute. The experts mostly use the first two methods. In each case the "pellet string" is spread over a short distance due to the movement of the gun muzzle as the shot exits the barrel. "Swing through" spreads the pellet string the most. But in either case it is a very small amount.

What a shooter is trying to do is swing the gun muzzle in such a manner so the "pellet string" is brought across the clay bird in flight. One author mentions to think of a paint-brush and you are taking a stroke across the target; "painting it with pellets." To do this requires a lot of practice but I think it is likely the best shooting method of the three.

So, "How can you use the TABLES to improve your trap shooting?"

There are dozens of "trap field" wind and weather situations. All you do is start by referring to the appropriate LEAD TABLE and then use this LEAD in the field to adjust as each situation dictates. No table is going to give you the advantage that several times a week trap shooting with some instruction will give you over the course of several months.

Trap shooting as a sport has a number of "fine tuning" features that are not the subject of this book. I advise you to buy a book on shooting trap and read it to sharpen your understanding of this very popular sport.

Please see below and on Page 84 for Trap Charts for ideal conditions.

Figure 1 - Typical Theoretical Trap LEADs at increasing distance – beginning at 17.5 yards with no wind. Read Distance Right to Left

Theoretical Trap LEAD
Ideal Conditions, Trap Loads

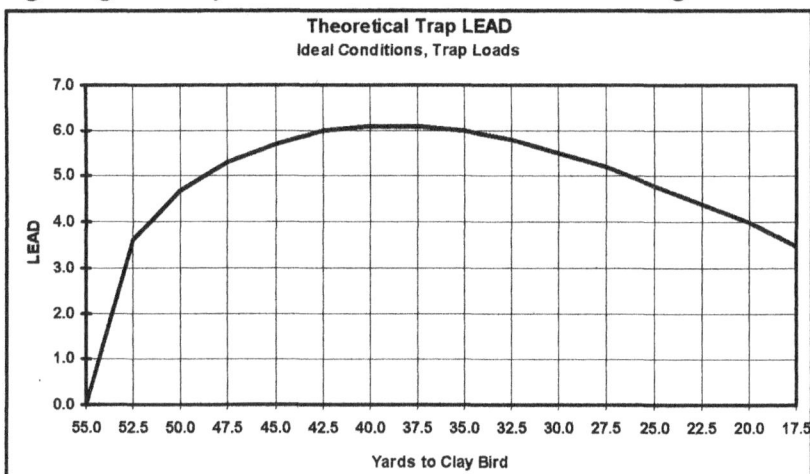

In Figure 1, illustrate how LEAD changes with distance as the Clay slows and then as velocity "dies" at the end of the Clay's flight from the launcher. Through the first half of the Clay flight the LEAD increases and throughout the last half of the flight the LEAD decreases. In "theory" a flushed

game bird "may" well present the same scenario. Please note the words "theory" and "may."

Of course it all depends; and that uncertainty is what makes for all the fun, and frustration!

Below in Figure 2, the chart scenario shows for a given "distance from the Clay" an idea as to what pattern spread is doing as the shot pellets travel the distances. And also what theoretical LEAD is doing at the same time. Also is the recommended "Kill zone" of 30 to 45 yards, that experts say is the best or optimum distance to break the clay.

Figure 2 – Theoretical LEADs at increasing distance- beginning at 17.5 yards no wind. Read Distance Right to Left.

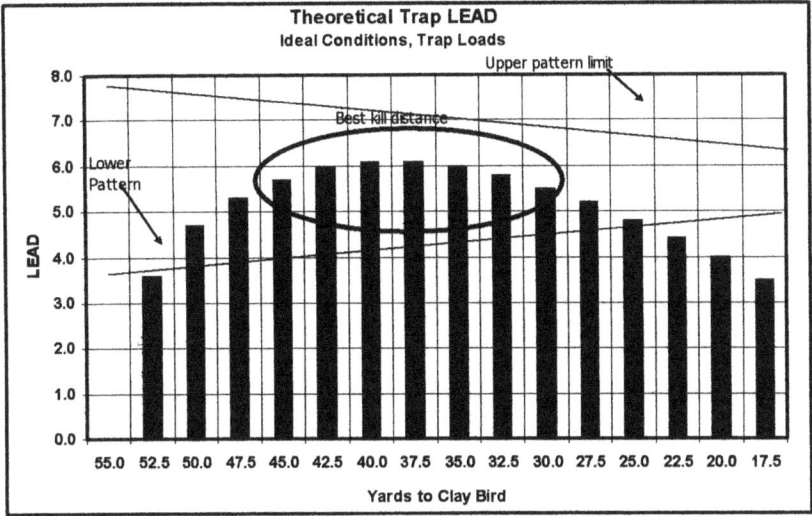

Theoretical Trap LEAD
Ideal Conditions, Trap Loads

Again the above two charts are a Theoretical representation under ideal conditions

Good shooting!

Chapter 15 - Finding Your "LEAD" From the Tables -

The following examples are from my "real life" shooting experiences. You likely have a couple of similar situations that you remember gave you some frustrating shooting opportunities. Try one or two examples of your own to test out how much LEAD you should be holding.

Example -
You are pass shooting doves. The day is beautiful and there is no wind. The doves are overhead at a distance of about 35 yards. They are flying at a speed you estimate at 50 miles per hour. You are shooting Field Load, # 7 1/2 lead shot pellets and you know the muzzle velocity is 1130 fps. You have shot about 10 rounds and have yet to hit a bird even though you are holding a strong LEAD of at least four feet.

Take a look at the LEAD-O-TABLE, Figure 1 on Page 88. Find the distance to the birds, at "35 yards" at the top of the chart and straight below this find the row marked "50 mph" on the left of the table. Where the "50 MPH" row and the "35 yard" column intersect you see the IDEAL LEAD of "9.0 feet."

All of a sudden you realize that your LEAD has been less than one half the distance needed. So by increasing your lead to around 9.0 feet you are now close to the required ideal LEAD.

If a miss is encountered by adjusting a foot or two either way, you can soon start recording hits.

This example is how using the LEAD-O-SLIDEs can give you some idea of how much to LEAD. In my mind this idea is worth a thousand words of "help from friends."

In a very real sense this example also describes my first experience with the notion of calculating LEADs. Such a procedure makes so much sense it almost defies our understanding to figure out WHY someone hasn't offered such an approach long before now.

But, no matter, here it is in black and white and with a little practice you too can come home with more birds or more kills on the Trap field.

LEAD-O-SLIDE Table 3

7-1/2 Lead Shot - 1130 fps Muzzle Velocity

Yards>	5	10	15	20	25	30	35	40	45	50	55	60
MPH	Read LEAD in Feet Below											
5	0.1	0.2	0.3	0.5	0.6	0.7	0.9	1.1	1.2	1.4	1.6	1.8
10	0.2	0.4	0.6	0.9	1.2	1.5	1.8	2.1	2.5	2.8	3.2	3.6
15	0.3	0.6	1.0	1.4	1.8	2.2	2.7	3.2	3.7	4.2	4.8	5.4
20	0.4	0.8	1.3	1.9	2.4	3.0	3.6	4.2	4.9	5.6	6.4	7.2
25	0.5	1.0	1.6	2.3	3.0	3.7	4.5	5.3	6.2	7.1	8.0	9.0
30	0.6	1.3	1.9	2.8	3.6	4.5	5.4	6.4	7.4	8.5	9.6	10.8
35	0.7	1.5	2.3	3.2	4.2	5.2	6.3	7.4	8.6	9.9	11.2	12.6
40	0.8	1.7	2.6	3.7	4.8	6.0	7.2	8.5	9.8	11.3	12.8	14.4
45	0.9	1.9	2.9	4.2	5.4	6.7	8.1	9.5	11.1	12.7	14.4	16.2
50	1.0	2.1	3.2	4.6	6.0	7.4	9.0	10.6	12.3	14.1	16.0	18.0
55	1.1	2.3	3.6	5.1	6.6	8.2	9.9	11.7	13.5	15.5	17.6	19.8
60	1.2	2.5	3.9	5.6	7.2	8.9	10.8	12.7	14.8	16.9	19.2	21.6

Figure 1

Chapter 16 - Using the LEAD-O-TABLES

Following there are LEAD-O-TABLES for different shot-shell pellet velocities common to factory or hand loaded lead pellet shot-shells. Also there are charts for steel pellet shot loads.

Shot velocity is the critical variable. Shot-shell length is one of the variables we can set aside. The shell is made longer so it can hold more ingredients; powder and shot. The more shot the less powder and vice versa, so velocities in the longer 3" and 3-1/2" shells vary accordingly.

Velocities of 1150 to 1250 fps are typical for field loads. Velocities of 1300 to 1550 fps are typical for "high brass" loads. Magnum loads can carry more shot weight, and as a result shot velocities are in the 1200 fps range but are "High Brass" due to the extra powder charge. You will notice that the LEAD differences do not vary all that much between TABLES for similar size shot that have similar muzzle velocities.

For instance for MV's (muzzle velocities) of around 1200 to 1250 fps (feet per second) in shot sizes 6, 7-1/2, 8, & 9 the LEADs do not vary that much. The

LEAD for a bird at 40 yards flying at 40 mph are 7.7 feet, 8.0 feet, 8.0 feet, & 8.3 feet respectively; a variation of only 6/10 of a foot or 7 inches at 40 yards.

At 40 yards the pattern diameter for a full choke barrel is 40 to 50 inches, 45 to 55 inches for a modified and over 6 feet for a cylinder bore.

The point? A TABLE close to your situation will be give you a LEAD close enough to assist in deciding your LEAD.

Similarly if you will look at the Tables or LEAD-O-TABLEs for the high brass shot velocities of around 1330 fps the same relationship occurs. For 2, 4, and 6 size pellets the LEAD for a bird at 40 mph at 40 yards are 6.7', 7.0', and 7.3'. A difference of 0.6 feet or 7 inches; again a small aiming difference with patterns in excess of 40 inches in diameter.

So you can see how I can suggest that the shot pattern will cover a lot of the "pure ballistics theory" considerations including shot drop. In addition, here is a way to make your LEAD Table reference time more manageable. If you are shooting field loads in combinations of shot sizes, selecting the LEAD-O-

TABLE for shot size 7-1/2, for size 6 through 9 shot and the LEAD-O-TABLE for shot size 4, the TABLE for size 2 through 6 will give you LEADs close enough.

Because of mass, the heavier shot gets there quicker than the lighter shot due to heavier shot's ability (mass) to overcome air resistance. A good rule of thumb is to avoid reading a LEAD from a chart that is more than two shot sizes different or more than 80 to 90 fps different in velocity than the load you are shooting.

Chapter 17 - The LEAD in Feet

In the LEAD-O-TABLES the LEAD is shown in feet and tenths. The following table will give you the inch reading for each tenth of a foot.

Tenths	Inches Rounded Off
0.1	1 inch
0.2	2 inches
0.3	4 inches
0.4	5 inches
0.5	6 inches
0.6	7 inches
0.7	8 inches
0.8	10 inches
0.9	11 inches

I simply read tenths as though they were inches and round off to the nearest foot for LEAD. This is another privilege shot pattern allows the shooter. For instance 9.4 feet I read as a LEAD of 9 feet, 9.6 feet I read as a LEAD of 10 feet. If you feel you are a very precise in your shooting you can use one-half foot increments. To attempt to use a LEAD closer than one-half foot increments is really unnecessary if not impossible from a practical viewpoint. But the numbers are there if you wish to try.

Chapter 18 - Selecting Your Table and the Velocity to Use

The tables are general in nature. The one factor that is likely to give a user of the LEAD-O-TABLEs the most difficulty is determining which muzzle velocity to use in looking up your IDEAL LEAD. All you need do is select a velocity for your pellet size. Most shotshell manufacturers supply brochures that give the muzzle velocity of their loads. Remember it is not necessary to know or use the "exact" pellet velocity because our friend "the spreading shot pellet pattern" works in our favor.

If you have a "low brass" field load lead pellet shotshell there are tables in the 1130 fps for 4's, 6's & 7-1/2's and an 1150 fps table for 8's & 9's. If you have a "high brass" shell then either it is either a magnum or a high velocity load. For magnum loads in lead there are 1250 fps tables for 2's, 4's, 6's, 8's & 7-1/2's and a 1200 fps table for # 9's. For high velocity loads the tables for all pellet sizes are for 1330 fps velocities. Also there are two tables for the 1450 and 1550 feet per second velocities. It would be best to treat these two velocities carefully and refer to the appropriate TABLE.

Data for developing the LEAD-O-TABLES for lead shot pellets are available from a number of shot-shell manufacturers. I did a cross check of data and found it all to be in close agreement. The muzzle velocities I have chosen are an average for low, medium and high velocity loads. Also there are dozens of different loads and shot-shell features within the industry. I have simplified the problem facing the average shooter by reducing the problem to three choices. This can properly be done because of our friend "the shot pellet pattern spread."

To use the tables you need only know if your shot-shell is "low brass" termed a "Field Load," "Magnum Load" or "High Velocity." The latter two are "high brass." The terms "low brass and high brass" are shooter terms describing the brass end of a shot-shell. Low and high are descriptive of how far the brass extends toward the muzzle end of the shell. The purpose of the additional brass on magnum and high velocity loads is simply to assist in containing the additional pressure resulting from the greater powder pressure in these loads as compared to the lower powder pressure field loads.

THE LEAD-O-TABLEs

LEAD-O-SLIDE	Table 1

 # 4 Lead Shot - 1130 fps Muzzle Velocity

Yards>	5	10	15	20	25	30	35	40	45	50	55	60
MPH	Read LEAD in Feet Below						Read LEAD in Feet Below					
0	0	0	0	0	0	0	0	0	0	0	0	0
5	0.1	0.2	0.3	0.4	0.6	0.7	0.8	1.0	1.1	1.3	1.5	1.6
10	0.2	0.4	0.6	0.9	1.1	1.4	1.7	2.0	2.3	2.6	2.9	3.3
15	0.3	0.6	0.9	1.3	1.7	2.1	2.5	3.0	3.4	3.9	4.4	4.9
20	0.4	0.8	1.3	1.8	2.3	2.8	3.4	4.0	4.6	5.2	5.9	5.5
25	0.5	1.0	1.6	2.2	2.9	3.5	4.2	4.9	5.7	6.5	7.3	8.2
30	0.6	1.2	1.9	2.7	3.4	4.2	5.1	4.9	6.8	7.8	8.8	9.8
35	0.7	1.4	2.2	3.1	4.0	4.9	5.9	6.9	8.0	9.1	10.2	11.5
40	0.8	1.6	2.5	3.6	4.6	5.6	6.7	7.9	9.1	10.4	11.7	13.1
45	0.9	1.8	2.8	4.0	5.1	6.3	7.6	8.9	10.3	11.7	13.2	14.7
50	1.0	2.1	3.2	4.5	5.7	7.0	8.4	9.9	11.4	13.0	14.6	16.4
55	1.1	2.3	3.5	4.9	6.3	7.7	9.3	10.9	12.5	14.3	16.1	18.0
60	1.2	2.5	3.8	5.3	6.9	8.4	10.1	11.9	13.7	15.6	17.6	19.6

LEAD-0-SLIDE	Table 2

 # 6 Lead Shot - 1130 fps Muzzle Velocity

Yards>	5	10	15	20	25	30	35	40	45	50	55	60
MPH	Read LEAD in Feet Below						Read LEAD in Feet Below					
0	0	0	0	0	0	0	0	0	0	0	0	0
5	0.1	0.2	0.3	0.5	0.6	0.7	0.9	1.0	1.2	1.4	1.5	1.7
10	0.2	0.4	0.6	0.9	1.2	1.4	1.7	2.0	2.4	2.7	3.1	3.4
15	0.3	0.6	1.0	1.4	1.8	2.2	2.6	3.1	3.6	4.1	4.6	5.2
20	0.4	0.8	1.3	1.8	2.3	2.9	3.5	4.1	4.7	5.4	6.1	6.9
25	0.5	1.0	1.6	2.3	2.9	3.6	4.3	5.1	5.9	6.8	7.7	8.6
30	0.6	1.2	1.9	2.7	3.5	4.3	5.2	6.1	7.1	8.1	9.2	10.3
35	0.7	1.4	2.2	3.2	4.1	5.1	6.1	7.2	8.3	9.5	10.7	12.0
40	0.8	1.7	2.6	3.6	4.7	5.8	7.0	8.2	9.5	10.8	12.2	13.7
45	0.9	1.9	2.9	4.1	5.3	6.5	7.8	9.2	10.7	12.2	13.8	15.5
50	1.0	2.1	3.2	4.5	5.9	7.2	8.7	10.2	11.8	13.5	15.3	17.2
55	1.1	2.3	3.5	5.0	6.4	8.0	9.6	11.2	13.0	14.9	16.8	18.9
60	1.2	2.5	3.8	5.5	7.0	8.7	10.4	12.3	14.2	16.2	18.4	20.6

LEAD-0-SLIDE		Table 3										
# 7-1/2 Lead Shot - 1130 fps Muzzle Velocity												
Yards>		5	10	15	20	25	30	35	40	45	50	55	60
MPH		Read LEAD in Feet Below						Read LEAD in Feet Below				
0	0	0	0	0	0	0	0	0	0	0	0	0	0
5	0.1	0.2	0.3	0.5	0.6	0.7	0.9	1.1	1.2	1.4	1.6	1.8
10	0.2	0.4	0.6	0.9	1.2	1.5	1.8	2.1	2.5	2.8	3.2	3.6
15	0.3	0.6	1.0	1.4	1.8	2.2	2.7	3.2	3.7	4.2	4.8	5.4
20	0.4	0.8	1.3	1.9	2.4	3.0	3.6	4.2	4.9	5.6	6.4	7.2
25	0.5	1.0	1.6	2.3	3.0	3.7	4.5	5.3	6.2	7.1	8.0	9.0
30	0.6	1.3	1.9	2.8	3.6	4.5	5.4	6.4	7.4	8.5	9.6	10.8
35	0.7	1.5	2.3	3.2	4.2	5.2	6.3	7.4	8.6	9.9	11.2	12.6
40	0.8	1.7	2.6	3.7	4.8	6.0	7.2	8.5	9.8	11.3	12.8	14.4
45	0.9	1.9	2.9	4.2	5.4	6.7	8.1	9.5	11.1	12.7	14.4	16.2
50	1.0	2.1	3.2	4.6	6.0	7.4	9.0	10.6	12.3	14.1	16.0	18.0
55	1.1	2.3	3.6	5.1	6.6	8.2	9.9	11.7	13.5	15.5	17.6	19.8
60	1.2	2.5	3.9	5.6	7.2	8.9	10.8	12.7	14.8	16.9	19.2	21.6

LEAD-0-SLIDE		Table 4											

 # 8 Lead Shot - 1150 fps Muzzle Velocity

Yards>	0	5	10	15	20	25	30	35	40	45	50	55	60
MPH	Read LEAD in Feet Below						Read LEAD in Feet Below						
0	0	0	0	0	0	0	0	0	0	0	0	0	0
5	0	0.1	0.2	0.3	0.5	0.6	0.7	0.9	1.1	1.2	1.4	1.6	1.8
10	0	0.2	0.4	0.6	0.9	1.2	1.5	1.8	2.1	2.5	2.8	3.2	3.6
15	0	0.3	0.6	1.0	1.4	1.8	2.2	2.7	3.2	3.7	4.3	4.8	5.5
20	0	0.4	0.8	1.3	1.8	2.4	3.0	3.6	4.2	4.9	5.7	6.5	7.3
25	0	0.5	1.0	1.6	2.3	3.0	3.7	4.5	5.3	6.2	7.1	8.1	9.1
30	0	0.6	1.2	1.9	2.8	3.6	4.5	5.4	6.4	7.4	8.5	9.7	10.9
35	0	0.7	1.4	2.2	3.2	4.2	5.2	6.3	7.4	8.6	9.9	11.3	12.7
40	0	0.8	1.6	2.6	3.7	4.8	5.9	7.2	8.5	9.9	11.4	12.9	14.6
45	0	0.9	1.9	2.9	4.2	5.4	6.7	8.1	9.6	11.1	12.8	14.5	16.4
50	0	1.0	2.1	3.2	4.6	6.0	7.4	9.0	10.6	12.4	14.2	16.1	18.2
55	0	1.1	2.3	3.5	5.1	6.6	8.2	9.9	11.7	13.6	15.6	17.8	20.0
60	0	1.2	2.5	3.8	5.5	7.2	8.9	10.8	12.7	14.8	17.0	19.4	21.8

LEAD-0-SLIDE **Table 5**

 # 9 Lead Shot - 1150 fps Muzzle Velocity

Yards>	5	10	15	20	25	30	35	40	45	50	55	60
MPH	Read LEAD in Feet Below					Read LEAD in Feet Below						
0	0	0	0	0	0	0	0	0	0	0	0	0
5	0.1	0.2	0.3	0.5	0.6	0.8	0.9	1.1	1.3	1.5	1.7	1.9
10	0.2	0.4	0.6	0.9	1.2	1.5	1.9	2.2	2.6	3.0	3.4	3.8
15	0.3	0.6	1.0	1.4	1.8	2.3	2.8	3.3	3.8	4.4	5.1	5.7
20	0.4	0.8	1.3	1.9	2.4	3.1	3.7	4.4	5.1	5.9	6.7	7.6
25	0.5	1.0	1.6	2.4	3.1	3.8	4.6	5.5	6.4	7.4	8.4	9.5
30	0.6	1.2	1.9	2.8	3.7	4.6	5.6	6.6	7.7	8.9	10.1	11.4
35	0.7	1.5	2.3	3.3	4.3	5.3	6.5	7.7	9.0	10.4	11.8	13.3
40	0.8	1.7	2.6	3.8	4.9	6.1	7.4	8.8	10.3	11.8	13.5	15.3
45	0.9	1.9	2.9	4.2	5.5	6.9	8.3	9.9	11.5	13.3	15.2	17.2
50	1.0	2.1	3.2	4.7	6.1	7.6	9.3	11.0	12.8	14.8	16.9	19.1
55	1.1	2.3	3.6	5.2	6.7	8.4	10.2	12.1	14.1	16.3	18.6	21.0
60	1.2	2.5	3.9	5.6	7.3	9.2	11.1	13.2	15.4	17.7	20.2	22.9

LEAD-0-SLIDE | **Table 6**

 # 2 Lead Shot - 1250 fps Muzzle Velocity

MPH \ Yards>	5	10	15	20	25	30	35	40	45	50	55	60
0	0	0	0	0	0	0	0	0	0	0	0	0
	Read LEAD in Feet Below						Read LEAD in Feet Below					
5	0.1	0.2	0.3	0.4	0.5	0.6	0.8	0.9	1.0	1.2	1.3	1.5
10	0.2	0.4	0.6	0.8	1.0	1.3	1.5	1.8	2.0	2.3	2.6	2.9
15	0.3	0.6	0.9	1.2	1.5	1.9	2.3	2.7	3.1	3.5	3.9	4.4
20	0.4	0.7	1.1	1.6	2.1	2.5	3.0	3.5	4.1	4.6	5.2	5.8
25	0.5	0.9	1.4	2.0	2.6	3.2	3.8	4.4	5.1	5.8	6.5	7.3
30	0.5	1.1	1.7	2.4	3.1	3.8	4.5	5.3	6.1	7.0	7.8	8.8
35	0.6	1.3	2.0	2.8	3.6	4.4	5.3	6.2	7.1	8.1	9.1	10.2
40	0.7	1.5	2.3	3.2	4.1	5.1	6.0	7.1	8.2	9.3	10.5	11.7
45	0.8	1.7	2.6	3.6	4.6	5.7	6.8	8.0	9.2	10.4	11.8	13.1
50	0.9	1.9	2.9	4.0	5.1	6.3	7.6	8.8	10.2	11.6	13.1	14.6
55	1.0	2.0	3.1	4.4	5.6	6.9	8.3	9.7	11.2	12.8	14.4	16.1
60	1.1	2.2	3.4	4.8	6.2	7.6	9.1	10.6	12.2	13.9	15.7	17.5

| LEAD-0-SLIDE | | Table 7 | | | | | | | | | | |

 # 4 Lead Shot - 1250 fps Muzzle Velocity

Yards>	5	10	15	20	25	30	35	40	45	50	55	60
MPH	Read LEAD in Feet Below					Read LEAD in Feet Below						
0	0	0	0	0	0	0	0	0	0	0	0	0
5	0.1	0.2	0.3	0.4	0.5	0.6	0.8	0.9	1.1	1.2	1.4	1.5
10	0.2	0.4	0.6	0.8	1.0	1.3	1.5	1.8	2.1	2.4	2.7	3.0
15	0.3	0.6	0.9	1.2	1.6	1.9	2.3	2.7	3.2	3.6	4.1	4.6
20	0.4	0.7	1.2	1.6	2.1	2.6	3.1	3.6	4.2	4.8	5.4	6.1
25	0.5	0.9	1.4	2.0	2.6	3.2	3.9	4.5	5.3	6.0	6.8	7.6
30	0.5	1.1	1.7	2.4	3.1	3.9	4.6	5.5	6.3	7.2	8.1	9.1
35	0.6	1.3	2.0	2.8	3.7	4.5	5.4	6.4	7.4	8.4	9.5	10.6
40	0.7	1.5	2.3	3.3	4.2	5.2	6.2	7.3	8.4	9.6	10.8	12.1
45	0.8	1.7	2.6	3.7	4.7	5.8	7.0	8.2	9.5	10.8	12.2	13.7
50	0.9	1.9	2.9	4.1	5.2	6.5	7.7	9.1	10.5	12.0	13.5	15.2
55	1.0	2.1	3.2	4.5	5.8	7.1	8.5	10.0	11.6	13.2	14.9	16.7
60	1.1	2.2	3.5	4.9	6.3	7.7	9.3	10.9	12.6	14.4	16.3	18.2

LEAD-0-SLIDE | **Table 8**

6 Lead Shot - 1250 fps Muzzzle Velocity

Yards>	5	10	15	20	25	30	35	40	45	50	55	60
MPH	Read LEAD in Feet Below						Read LEAD in Feet Below					
0	0	0	0	0	0	0	0	0	0	0	0	0
5	0.1	0.2	0.3	0.4	0.5	0.7	0.8	0.9	1.1	1.3	1.4	1.6
10	0.2	0.4	0.6	0.8	1.1	1.3	1.6	1.9	2.2	2.5	2.9	3.2
15	0.3	0.6	0.9	1.3	1.6	2.0	2.4	2.8	3.3	3.8	4.3	4.8
20	0.4	0.8	1.2	1.7	2.2	2.7	3.2	3.8	4.4	5.0	5.7	6.4
25	0.5	0.9	1.5	2.1	2.7	3.3	4.0	4.7	5.5	6.3	7.1	8.0
30	0.5	1.1	1.8	2.5	3.2	4.0	4.8	5.7	6.6	7.6	8.6	9.6
35	0.6	1.3	2.0	2.9	3.8	4.7	5.6	6.6	7.7	8.8	10.0	11.2
40	0.7	1.5	2.3	3.3	4.3	5.3	6.4	7.6	8.8	10.1	11.4	12.8
45	0.8	1.7	2.6	3.8	4.8	6.0	7.2	8.5	9.9	11.3	12.9	14.4
50	0.9	1.9	2.9	4.2	5.4	6.7	8.0	9.5	11.0	12.6	14.3	16.0
55	1.0	2.1	3.2	4.6	5.9	7.3	8.8	10.4	12.1	13.9	15.7	17.7
60	1.1	2.3	3.5	5.0	6.5	8.0	9.6	11.4	13.2	15.1	17.1	19.3

LEAD-0-SLIDE		Table 9										

 # 7-1/2 Lead Shot - 1250 fps Muzzle Velocity

Yards>	5	10	15	20	25	30	35	40	45	50	55	60
MPH	Read LEAD in Feet Below					Read LEAD in Feet Below						
0	0	0	0	0	0	0	0	0	0	0	0	0
5	0.1	0.2	0.3	0.4	0.6	0.7	0.8	1.0	1.1	1.3	1.5	1.7
10	0.2	0.4	0.6	0.9	1.1	1.4	1.7	2.0	2.3	2.6	3.0	3.4
15	0.3	0.6	0.9	1.3	1.7	2.1	2.5	3.0	3.4	4.0	4.5	5.1
20	0.4	0.8	1.2	1.7	2.2	2.8	3.3	3.9	4.6	5.3	6.0	6.8
25	0.5	0.9	1.5	2.1	2.8	3.4	4.2	4.9	5.7	6.6	7.5	8.5
30	0.5	1.1	1.8	2.6	3.3	4.1	5.0	5.9	6.9	7.9	9.0	10.2
35	0.6	1.3	2.1	3.0	3.9	4.8	5.8	6.9	8.0	9.2	10.5	11.9
40	0.7	1.5	2.4	3.4	4.4	5.5	6.7	7.9	9.2	10.6	12.0	13.6
45	0.8	1.7	2.7	3.8	5.0	6.2	7.5	8.9	10.3	11.9	13.5	15.2
50	0.9	1.9	3.0	4.3	5.5	6.9	8.3	9.9	11.5	13.2	15.0	16.9
55	1.0	2.1	3.3	4.7	6.1	7.6	9.2	10.8	12.6	14.5	16.5	18.6
60	1.1	2.3	3.5	5.1	6.6	8.3	10.0	11.8	13.8	15.8	18.0	20.3

LEAD-O-SLIDE		Table 10										

8 Lead Shot - 1250 fps Muzzle Velocity

Yards>	5	10	15	20	25	30	35	40	45	50	55	60
MPH	Read LEAD in Feet Below						Read LEAD in Feet Below					
0	0	0	0	0	0	0	0	0	0	0	0	0
5	0.1	0.2	0.3	0.4	0.6	0.7	0.8	1.0	1.2	1.3	1.5	1.7
10	0.2	0.4	0.6	0.9	1.1	1.4	1.7	2.0	2.3	2.7	3.1	3.5
15	0.3	0.6	0.9	1.3	1.7	2.1	2.5	3.0	3.5	4.0	4.6	5.2
20	0.4	0.8	1.2	1.7	2.2	2.8	3.4	4.0	4.7	5.4	6.2	6.9
25	0.5	1.0	1.5	2.2	2.8	3.5	4.2	5.0	5.9	6.7	7.7	8.7
30	0.5	1.1	1.8	2.6	3.4	4.2	5.1	6.0	7.0	8.1	9.2	10.4
35	0.6	1.3	2.1	3.0	3.9	4.9	5.9	7.0	8.2	9.4	10.8	12.2
40	0.7	1.5	2.4	3.4	4.5	5.6	6.8	8.0	9.4	10.8	12.3	13.9
45	0.8	1.7	2.7	3.9	5.0	6.3	7.6	9.0	10.5	12.1	13.8	15.6
50	0.9	1.9	3.0	4.3	5.6	7.0	8.5	10.0	11.7	13.5	15.4	17.4
55	1.0	2.1	3.3	4.7	6.2	7.7	9.3	11.0	12.9	14.8	16.9	19.1
60	1.1	2.3	3.6	5.2	6.7	8.4	10.2	12.0	14.1	16.2	18.5	20.8

LEAD-O-SLIDE		Table 11											
# 9 Lead Shot - 1200 fps Muzzle Velocity													
Yards>													
MPH	5	10	15	20	25	30	35	40	45	50	55	60
0	0	0	0	0	0	0	0	0	0	0	0	0
5	0.1	0.2	0.3	0.5	0.6	0.7	0.9	1.1	1.2	1.4	1.6	1.9
10	0.2	0.4	0.6	0.9	1.2	1.5	1.8	2.1	2.5	2.9	3.3	3.7
15	0.3	0.6	0.9	1.4	1.8	2.2	2.7	3.2	3.7	4.3	4.9	5.6
20	0.4	0.8	1.2	1.8	2.4	3.0	3.6	4.3	5.0	5.8	6.6	7.5
25	0.5	1.0	1.6	2.3	3.0	3.7	4.5	5.3	6.2	7.2	8.2	9.3
30	0.6	1.2	1.9	2.7	3.6	4.4	5.4	6.4	7.5	8.6	9.9	11.2
35	0.7	1.4	2.2	3.2	4.1	5.2	6.3	7.5	8.7	10.1	11.5	13.0
40	0.8	1.6	2.5	3.6	4.7	5.9	7.2	8.5	10.0	11.5	13.2	14.9
45	0.9	1.8	2.8	4.1	5.3	6.7	8.1	9.6	11.2	13.0	14.8	16.8
50	1.0	2.0	3.1	4.5	5.9	7.4	9.0	10.7	12.5	14.4	16.5	18.6
55	1.1	2.2	3.4	5.0	6.5	8.1	9.9	11.7	13.7	15.9	18.1	20.5
60	1.1	2.4	3.7	5.5	7.1	8.9	10.8	12.8	15.0	17.3	19.7	22.4

Read LEAD in Feet Below

LEAD-O-SLIDE		Table 12										

 # 2 Lead Shot - 1330 fps Muzzle Velocity

Yards>	5	10	15	20	25	30	35	40	45	50	55	60
MPH	Read LEAD in Feet Below					Read LEAD in Feet Below						
0	0	0	0	0	0	0	0	0	0	0	0	0
5	0.1	0.2	0.3	0.4	0.5	0.6	0.7	0.8	1.0	1.1	1.3	1.4
10	0.2	0.3	0.5	0.8	1.0	1.2	1.4	1.7	1.9	2.2	2.5	2.8
15	0.3	0.5	0.8	1.1	1.5	1.8	2.2	2.5	2.9	3.3	3.8	4.2
20	0.3	0.7	1.1	1.5	1.9	2.4	2.9	3.4	3.9	4.4	5.0	5.6
25	0.4	0.9	1.3	1.9	2.4	3.0	3.6	4.2	4.9	5.5	6.3	7.0
30	0.5	1.0	1.6	2.3	2.9	3.6	4.3	5.1	5.8	6.7	7.5	8.4
35	0.6	1.2	1.9	2.7	3.4	4.2	5.0	5.9	6.8	7.8	8.8	9.8
40	0.7	1.4	2.2	3.0	3.9	4.8	5.8	6.7	7.8	8.9	10.0	11.2
45	0.8	1.6	2.4	3.4	4.4	5.4	6.5	7.6	8.8	10.0	11.3	12.6
50	0.9	1.7	2.7	3.8	4.9	6.0	7.2	8.4	9.7	11.1	12.5	14.0
55	0.9	1.9	3.0	4.2	5.4	6.6	7.9	9.3	10.7	12.2	13.8	15.4
60	1.0	2.1	3.2	4.6	5.8	7.2	8.6	10.1	11.7	13.3	15.0	16.8

LEAD-0-SLIDE **Table 13**

4 Lead Shot - 1330 fps Muzzle Velocity

Read LEAD in Feet Below

Yards>	5	10	15	20	25	30	35	40	45	50	55	60
MPH												
0	0	0	0	0	0	0	0	0	0	0	0	0
5	0.1	0.2	0.3	0.4	0.5	0.6	0.7	0.9	1.0	1.1	1.3	1.5
10	0.2	0.4	0.5	0.8	1.0	1.2	1.5	1.7	2.0	2.3	2.6	2.9
15	0.3	0.5	0.8	1.2	1.5	1.8	2.2	2.6	3.0	3.4	3.9	4.4
20	0.3	0.7	1.1	1.5	2.0	2.5	3.0	3.5	4.0	4.6	5.2	5.8
25	0.4	0.9	1.4	1.9	2.5	3.1	3.7	4.3	5.0	5.7	6.5	7.3
30	0.5	1.1	1.6	2.3	3.0	3.7	4.4	5.2	6.0	6.9	7.8	8.8
35	0.6	1.2	1.9	2.7	3.5	4.3	5.2	6.1	7.0	8.0	9.1	10.2
40	0.7	1.4	2.2	3.1	4.0	4.9	5.9	7.0	8.0	9.2	10.4	11.7
45	0.8	1.6	2.4	3.5	4.5	5.5	6.6	7.8	9.1	10.3	11.7	13.1
50	0.9	1.8	2.7	3.9	5.0	6.1	7.4	8.7	10.1	11.5	13.0	14.6
55	0.9	1.9	3.0	4.2	5.5	6.8	8.1	9.6	11.1	12.6	14.3	16.0
60	1.0	2.1	3.3	4.6	6.0	7.4	8.9	10.4	12.1	13.8	15.6	17.5

LEAD-0-SLIDE		Table 14										

 # 6 Lead Shot - 1330 fps Muzzle Velocity

Yards>	5	10	15	20	25	30	35	40	45	50	55	60
MPH	Read LEAD in Feet Below											
0	0	0	0	0	0	0	0	0	0	0	0	0
5	0.1	0.2	0.3	0.4	0.5	0.6	0.8	0.9	1.1	1.2	1.4	1.5
10	0.2	0.4	0.6	0.8	1.0	1.3	1.5	1.8	2.1	2.4	2.7	3.1
15	0.3	0.5	0.8	1.2	1.5	1.9	2.3	2.7	3.2	3.6	4.1	4.6
20	0.3	0.7	1.1	1.6	2.0	2.5	3.1	3.6	4.2	4.8	5.5	6.2
25	0.4	0.9	1.4	2.0	2.6	3.2	3.8	4.5	5.3	6.1	6.9	7.7
30	0.5	1.1	1.7	2.4	3.1	3.8	4.6	5.4	6.3	7.3	8.2	9.3
35	0.6	1.2	1.9	2.8	3.6	4.5	5.4	6.3	7.4	8.5	9.6	10.8
40	0.7	1.4	2.2	3.2	4.1	5.1	6.1	7.3	8.4	9.7	11.0	12.4
45	0.8	1.6	2.5	3.6	4.6	5.7	6.9	8.2	9.5	10.9	12.4	13.9
50	0.9	1.8	2.8	4.0	5.1	6.4	7.7	9.1	10.5	12.1	13.7	15.5
55	0.9	2.0	3.0	4.4	5.6	7.0	8.4	10.0	11.6	13.3	15.1	17.0
60	1.0	2.1	3.3	4.8	6.1	7.6	9.2	10.9	12.7	14.5	16.5	18.6

LEAD-0-SLIDE	Table 15

7-1/2 Lead Shot - 1330 fps Muzzle Velocity

Read LEAD in Feet Below

Yards> MPH	5	10	15	20	25	30	35	40	45	50	55	60
0	0	0	0	0	0	0	0	0	0	0	0	0
5	0.1	0.2	0.3	0.4	0.5	0.7	0.8	0.9	1.1	1.3	1.4	1.6
10	0.2	0.4	0.6	0.8	1.1	1.3	1.6	1.9	2.2	2.5	2.9	3.3
15	0.3	0.5	0.8	1.2	1.6	2.0	2.4	2.8	3.3	3.8	4.3	4.9
20	0.3	0.7	1.1	1.6	2.1	2.6	3.2	3.8	4.4	5.1	5.8	6.5
25	0.4	0.9	1.4	2.0	2.6	3.3	4.0	4.7	5.5	6.3	7.2	8.2
30	0.5	1.1	1.7	2.4	3.2	3.9	4.8	5.7	6.6	7.6	8.7	9.8
35	0.6	1.3	2.0	2.8	3.7	4.6	5.6	6.6	7.7	8.9	10.1	11.4
40	0.7	1.4	2.2	3.2	4.2	5.3	6.4	7.6	8.8	10.2	11.6	13.1
45	0.8	1.6	2.5	3.6	4.7	5.9	7.2	8.5	9.9	11.4	13.0	14.7
50	0.9	1.8	2.8	4.1	5.3	6.6	8.0	9.4	11.0	12.7	14.5	16.3
55	0.9	2.0	3.1	4.5	5.8	7.2	8.8	10.4	12.1	14.0	15.9	18.0
60	1.0	2.2	3.4	4.9	6.3	7.9	9.6	11.3	13.2	15.2	17.4	19.6

Data used to develop the LEAD Tables for steel shot was not as abundant as that for lead but I do feel that the data available are representative of what the shot-shell industry is offering and will provide you with LEAD information within a few inches of the IDEAL LEAD. In steel shot pellets I have used velocities of 1260, 1370, 1450, and 1550 feet per second.

The latter two velocities are given to encompass the newer higher velocity loads in steel. Chose the TABLE closet to your advertised velocity and you will do fine.

For instance, I have a box of 3-1/2" Federal Copper Coated BB Magnum loads that have a muzzle velocity noted on the box of 1350 fps. In this case I would use the 1370 velocity tables.

LEAD-O-SLIDE		Table 16										

 # T, BBB, BB & 2 Steel Shot - 1260 fps Muzzle Velocity

Yards>	5	10	15	20	25	30	35	40	45	50	55	60
MPH	Read LEAD in Feet Below						Read LEAD in Feet Below					
0	0	0	0	0	0	0	0	0	0	0	0	0
5	0.1	0.2	0.3	0.4	0.5	0.6	0.7	0.8	1.0	1.1	1.2	1.4
10	0.2	0.4	0.6	0.8	1.0	1.2	1.5	1.7	1.9	2.2	2.5	2.8
15	0.3	0.5	0.8	1.2	1.5	1.8	2.2	2.5	2.9	3.3	3.7	4.1
20	0.4	0.7	1.1	1.6	2.0	2.4	2.9	3.4	3.9	4.4	5.0	5.5
25	0.4	0.9	1.4	1.9	2.5	3.0	3.6	4.2	4.9	5.5	6.2	6.9
30	0.5	1.1	1.7	2.3	3.0	3.7	4.4	5.1	5.8	6.6	7.4	8.3
35	0.6	1.3	2.0	2.7	3.5	4.3	5.1	5.9	6.8	7.7	8.7	9.7
40	0.7	1.5	2.2	3.1	4.0	4.9	5.8	6.8	7.8	8.8	9.9	11.0
45	0.8	1.6	2.5	3.5	4.5	5.5	6.5	7.6	8.8	9.9	11.1	12.4
50	0.9	1.8	2.8	3.9	5.0	6.1	7.3	8.5	9.7	11.0	12.4	13.8
55	1.0	2.0	3.1	4.3	5.5	6.7	8.0	9.3	10.7	12.1	13.6	15.2
60	1.1	2.2	3.4	4.7	6.0	7.3	8.7	10.2	11.7	13.2	14.9	16.5

LEAD-0-SLIDE	Table 17

4 & 6 Steel Shot - 1260 fps Muzzle Velocity

Yards>	5	10	15	20	25	30	35	40	45	50	55	60
MPH	Read LEAD in Feet Below					Read LEAD in Feet Below						
0	0	0	0	0	0	0	0	0	0	0	0	0
5	0.1	0.2	0.3	0.4	0.5	0.7	0.8	0.9	1.1	1.3	1.4	1.6
10	0.2	0.4	0.6	0.8	1.1	1.3	1.6	1.9	2.2	2.5	2.9	3.2
15	0.3	0.6	0.9	1.2	1.6	2.0	2.4	2.8	3.3	3.8	4.3	4.8
20	0.4	0.7	1.2	1.7	2.1	2.7	3.2	3.8	4.4	5.1	5.7	6.5
25	0.5	0.9	1.5	2.1	2.7	3.3	4.0	4.7	5.5	6.3	7.2	8.1
30	0.5	1.1	1.7	2.5	3.2	4.0	4.8	5.7	6.6	7.6	8.6	9.7
35	0.6	1.3	2.0	2.9	3.8	4.7	5.6	6.6	7.7	8.8	10.0	11.3
40	0.7	1.5	2.3	3.3	4.3	5.3	6.4	7.6	8.8	10.1	11.5	12.9
45	0.8	1.7	2.6	3.7	4.8	6.0	7.2	8.5	9.9	11.4	12.9	14.5
50	0.9	1.9	2.9	4.2	5.4	6.7	8.0	9.5	11.0	12.6	14.3	16.1
55	1.0	2.1	3.2	4.6	5.9	7.3	8.8	10.4	12.1	13.9	15.8	17.7
60	1.1	2.2	3.5	5.0	6.4	8.0	9.6	11.4	13.2	15.2	17.2	19.4

LEAD-0-SLIDE Table 18

T, BBB, BB & 2 Steel Shot - 1370 fps Muzzle Velocity

MPH \ Yards>	5	10	15	20	25	30	35	40	45	50	55	60
	Read LEAD in Feet Below											
0	0	0	0	0	0	0	0	0	0	0	0	0
5	0.1	0.2	0.3	0.4	0.5	0.6	0.7	0.8	0.9	1.0	1.1	1.3
10	0.2	0.3	0.5	0.7	0.9	1.1	1.3	1.6	1.8	2.0	2.3	2.5
15	0.2	0.5	0.8	1.1	1.4	1.7	2.0	2.3	2.7	3.0	3.4	3.8
20	0.3	0.7	1.0	1.4	1.8	2.2	2.7	3.1	3.6	4.0	4.5	5.0
25	0.4	0.8	1.3	1.8	2.3	2.8	3.3	3.9	4.5	5.1	5.7	6.3
30	0.5	1.0	1.5	2.1	2.7	3.4	4.0	4.7	5.3	6.1	6.8	7.6
35	0.6	1.2	1.8	2.5	3.2	3.9	4.7	5.4	6.2	7.1	7.9	8.8
40	0.7	1.3	2.1	2.9	3.6	4.5	5.3	6.2	7.1	8.1	9.1	10.1
45	0.7	1.5	2.3	3.2	4.1	5.0	6.0	7.0	8.0	9.1	10.2	11.4
50	0.8	1.7	2.6	3.6	4.6	5.6	6.7	7.8	8.9	10.1	11.3	12.6
55	0.9	1.8	2.8	3.9	5.0	6.1	7.3	8.5	9.8	11.1	12.5	13.9
60	1.0	2.0	3.1	4.3	5.5	6.7	8.0	9.3	10.7	12.1	13.6	15.1

LEAD-0-SLIDE	Table 19											

 # 4 & 6 Steel Shot - 1370 fps Muzzle Velocity

MPH \ Yards>	5	10	15	20	25	30	35	40	45	50	55	60
	Read LEAD in Feet Below					Read LEAD in Feet Below						
0	0	0	0	0	0	0	0	0	0	0	0	0
5	0.1	0.2	0.3	0.4	0.5	0.6	0.7	0.9	1.0	1.2	1.3	1.5
10	0.2	0.3	0.5	0.8	1.0	1.2	1.5	1.7	2.0	2.3	2.6	2.9
15	0.2	0.5	0.8	1.1	1.5	1.8	2.2	2.6	3.0	3.5	3.9	4.4
20	0.3	0.7	1.1	1.5	2.0	2.4	2.9	3.5	4.0	4.6	5.2	5.9
25	0.4	0.9	1.3	1.9	2.5	3.0	3.7	4.3	5.0	5.8	6.5	7.3
30	0.5	1.0	1.6	2.3	2.9	3.7	4.4	5.2	6.0	6.9	7.8	8.8
35	0.6	1.2	1.9	2.7	3.4	4.3	5.1	6.1	7.0	8.1	9.1	10.3
40	0.7	1.4	2.1	3.0	3.9	4.9	5.9	6.9	8.0	9.2	10.4	11.7
45	0.7	1.5	2.4	3.4	4.4	5.5	6.6	7.8	9.0	10.4	11.7	13.2
50	0.8	1.7	2.7	3.8	4.9	6.1	7.3	8.7	10.0	11.5	13.1	14.7
55	0.9	1.9	2.9	4.2	5.4	6.7	8.1	9.5	11.0	12.7	14.4	16.1
60	1.0	2.1	3.2	4.6	5.9	7.3	8.8	10.4	12.1	13.8	15.7	17.6

LEAD-O-SLIDE	Table 20											
# T, BBB, BB & 2 Steel Shot - 1450 fps Muzzle Velocity												
Yards>	0	5	10	15	20	25	30	35	40	45	50	55	60
MPH		Read LEAD in Feet Below					Read LEAD in Feet Below						
0	0	0	0	0	0	0	0	0	0	0	0	0	0
5		0.1	0.2	0.2	0.3	0.4	0.5	0.6	0.7	0.8	1.0	1.1	1.2
10		0.2	0.3	0.5	0.7	0.9	1.1	1.3	1.5	1.7	1.9	2.1	2.4
15		0.2	0.5	0.7	1.0	1.3	1.6	1.9	2.2	2.5	2.9	3.2	3.6
20		0.3	0.6	1.0	1.4	1.7	2.1	2.5	2.9	3.4	3.8	4.3	4.8
25		0.4	0.8	1.2	1.7	2.2	2.6	3.1	3.7	4.2	4.8	5.4	6.0
30		0.5	0.9	1.5	2.0	2.6	3.2	3.8	4.4	5.1	5.7	6.4	7.1
35		0.5	1.1	1.7	2.4	3.0	3.7	4.4	5.1	5.9	6.7	7.5	8.3
40		0.6	1.3	1.9	2.7	3.4	4.2	5.0	5.9	6.7	7.6	8.6	9.5
45		0.7	1.4	2.2	3.0	3.9	4.8	5.7	6.6	7.6	8.6	9.6	10.7
50		0.8	1.6	2.4	3.4	4.3	5.3	6.3	7.3	8.4	9.5	10.7	11.9
55		0.9	1.7	2.7	3.7	4.7	5.8	6.9	8.1	9.3	10.5	11.8	13.1
60		0.9	1.9	2.9	4.1	5.2	6.3	7.5	8.8	10.1	11.5	12.9	14.3

LEAD-0-SLIDE   Table 21

 # T, BBB, BB & 2 Steel Shot - 1550 fps Muzzle Velocity

Read LEAD in Feet Below

MPH / Yards>	0	5	10	15	20	25	30	35	40	45	50	55	60
0	0	0	0	0	0	0	0	0	0	0	0	0	0
5	0	0.1	0.1	0.2	0.3	0.4	0.5	0.6	0.7	0.8	0.9	1.0	1.1
10	0	0.1	0.3	0.5	0.6	0.8	1.0	1.2	1.4	1.6	1.8	2.0	2.2
15	0	0.2	0.4	0.7	0.9	1.2	1.5	1.8	2.1	2.4	2.7	3.0	3.3
20	0	0.3	0.6	0.9	1.3	1.6	2.0	2.4	2.7	3.1	3.6	4.0	4.5
25	0	0.4	0.7	1.1	1.6	2.0	2.5	2.9	3.4	3.9	4.5	5.0	5.6
30	0	0.4	0.9	1.4	1.9	2.4	3.0	3.5	4.1	4.7	5.4	6.0	6.7
35	0	0.5	1.0	1.6	2.2	2.8	3.5	4.1	4.8	5.5	6.2	7.0	7.8
40	0	0.6	1.2	1.8	2.5	3.2	4.0	4.7	5.5	6.3	7.1	8.0	8.9
45	0	0.7	1.3	2.0	2.8	3.6	4.4	5.3	6.2	7.1	8.0	9.0	10.0
50	0	0.7	1.5	2.3	3.2	4.0	4.9	5.9	6.9	7.9	8.9	10.0	11.1
55	0	0.8	1.6	2.5	3.5	4.4	5.4	6.5	7.5	8.7	9.8	11.0	12.3
60	0	0.9	1.8	2.7	3.8	4.8	5.9	7.1	8.2	9.4	10.7	12.0	13.4

LEAD-O-TABLE Chart Family

The last chart in Wing Shooting LEAD is one to give you in one glance all the charts with LEADs at five distances, 20, 30, 40, 50 and 60 yards. I do this to give you a feel for what happens and to realize it is not as dramatic as it is natural. When you see the Family Chart you all of a sudden realize it is merely a progression. More velocity and weight adds up to less LEAD.

As you examine the TABLEs in detail you will find that shot size and weight does make a difference in LEAD. The smallest LEADs go to the fastest and the heaviest; the "fastest" because it simply gets there quicker and the "heaviest" because it can overcome wind resistance more easily.

On the next page you will see what I mean. Note the curve in the lines. This is due to the loss in velocity due to wind resistance. If you were shooting in a vacuum the lines would be straight. Notice also at 50 yards there is a good seven foot difference in LEAD required from the slowest to the fastest loads. The Laws of Physics do apply and from them we can at least know more about LEAD than before! Have fun!

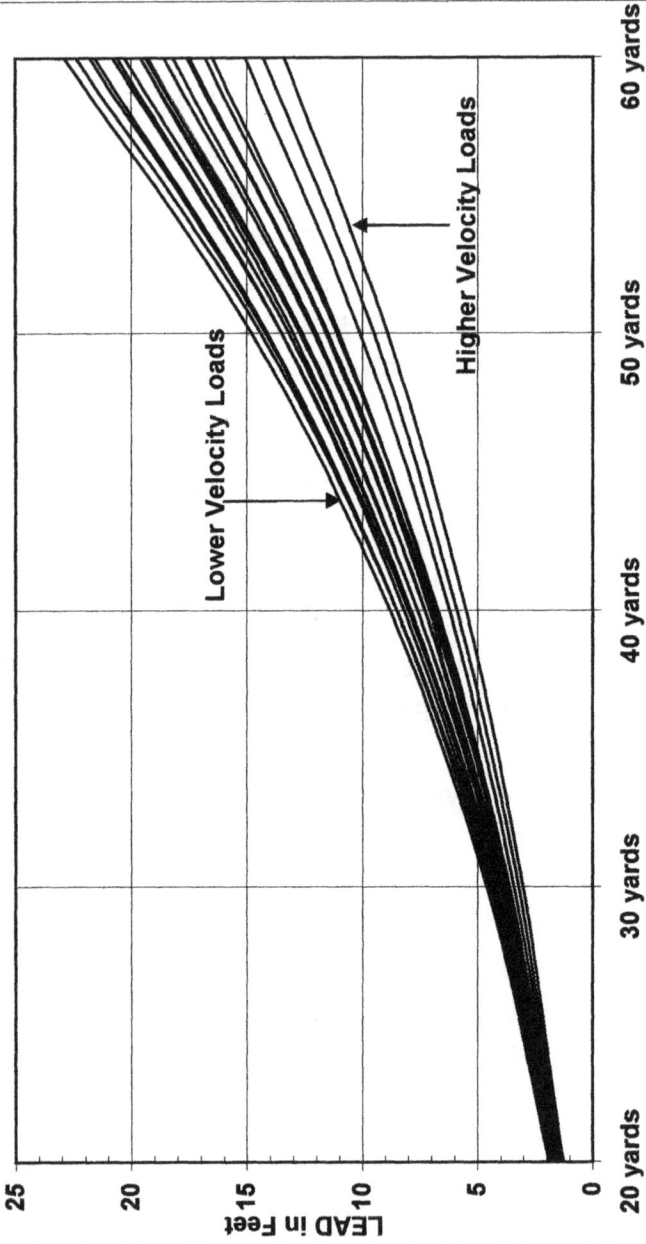

LEAD Curve Family for Game Birds - all loads

Lower Velocity Loads

Higher Velocity Loads

LEAD in Feet

25
20
15
10
5
0

20 yards
30 yards
40 yards
50 yards
60 yards